TANTRISM IN NEPAL

Contact Address of the Author
Vidya Bahadur Bajracharya
Bajra Teaching Service, wotu,
guchhatole (Sabal Bahal),
Ward No. 24, House No 45 (ka),
Kathmandu, Nepal
Telephone No. : 4249053, 4249608

TANTRISM IN NEPAL

Vidya Bahadur Bajracharya

ADROIT PUBLISHERS

Published by
ADROIT PUBLISHERS
4675/21, Ganpati Bhawan, Ansari Road,
Daryaganj, New Delhi-110 002
Phones : 011-23266030, 55302465

Distributors
AKHIL BOOK DISTRIBUTORS
e-mail: akhilbooks@yahoo.com
akhilbooks@hotmail.com

ISBN : 81-87392-62-2

Layout
Sudhir Vatsa

Laser Typeset by
Nidhi Laser Point
e-mail: nidhi_vatsa@hotmail.com

Printed in India on behalf of M/s Adroit Publishers by
Arpit Printographers, B-7, Saraswati Complex,
Subhash Chowk, Laxmi Nagar, Delhi-110 092
Phones : 09350809192, 011-30971860

Dedicated to all those people who have high interest in this field.

—V.B. Bajracharya

CONTENTS

PREFACE

My this book 'Tantrism in Nepal' solely and wholly is the product of my pretty fourteen years research work and innovative practice or experiment of more than twenty years. In the period of fourteen years Research, I have peeped into Hinduism and Buddhism to know their role in the field of tantric application in various walks and turnings of human life. I know it that every religion whether it is Hinduism or Buddhism or other religion has their tantric strength because of existence of many gods and goddesses and their divine power. Those gods and goddesses of power generate their high power in humanity to reward or punish the human beings for their good and bad activities. In the course of my research, I have studied the existence of evil spirits and many kinds of bad black spirits and their trouble offering, pain and problem creating activites in the life of the people. I have moved here and there-sometimes to the graves and sometimes to the temples, inns, pilgrim etc to collect knowledge about how those harmful evil spirits and black spirits are controlled and how suffering people are healed. when I was busy in my research on the way I found that Nepalese people are highly influenced by these evil spirits and black spirits. People are suffering much from such spirits. So they are supposed as human fate turners. It also I found out that the sufferers are healed by healers by using their tantric power. From my research work it has been clear that there are exitence of evil spirits and black spirit such as witches, wizards, ghosts and many kinds of shadowy figures. The shadowy evil spirits are catagorised as fantoms and gonams. I have mentioned such shadowy figures in many places in this book. They, time to time, appear in the human doors and create pain and problem in human life. I found that people are afraid of such spirits. Persons who suffer from such evil beings visit to sages, monks, hermits, Dhami, jhakre etc to get relief from suffering and to be safe from such harmful spirits. But the people who have not been victim to such spirits laugh at the people when they hear about such evil spirits. But it is the fact that the existence of such harmful and fearful spirits is true that move scattering many ugly events in the human world. Such uncommon spirits are still roaming to many parts of the world causing pain and problem in human doors since centuries. Such harmful evil spirits and black spirits fly invisibly and appear time to time unexpectedly in people's home to prevail abnormal situation around the dwelling area. It is also I found out that such evil spirits and black spirits mostly appear at night in old and delapidated houses. It also I want to make the people know that on the way to my Research I have got chance to see harmful spirits as ghosts, black fantiom (khyak) witches, wizards etc. When I had visited to different possible centres of such spirits. I have visited to grave or tumb, Inns, public lodges (Dharmashala), temples of the country in different time to get rigid evidence or proof. Keen observation and critical thinking are done to know more about such spirits, their power, their way or style of existence. It also I found out that Hindusim and Buddhism have vital role as their tantric calebre to control such harmful evil spirits and black spirits. There are many gods and goddesses of power in these religions. They have played great role to control evil activities of evil beings by using their divine power. The healers of unknown diseases also holding ritual performance, borrow divine power and use it as uncomman strength to put away and to weaken the power of evil spirits. So main sources of heading of the diseases caused by harmful evil and black spirits is the gods and goddesses of power. All the things of power mentioned in the religions is divine power is used by the healer and trouble creators for their tantrtic benefit.

Religion and science are two wings of human life. What one wing can do that can't be done by another wing. What religion can do can't be done by science vice-versa both have their own pecularties. Both have their own antagonistic qualities. Religion is older than science has deductive style where as science is younger and modern in style and has new inductive method. One is virtical and another is horizental one deals with soul and another deals with body. Religion is for vritue can't be seen and measured for its accurate value. But science is practical can be seen and early measured and also can be valued accurately. Tantrism is religious product. So it can't be correctly valued. Most of the product of tantrism is abstract and subjective in quality. It's effect differs differently for different persons. So valuation and measurement of tantric events and actions should be done seperately. But in practical life majority of people are suffering much due to their over belief in super power of gods and goddesses as well as falling into depth of superstition. Evil spirits and black spirits appear off and on in human residence and throw there a little evil Power for the people. But people think it much. People have to take it as great trouble in the life. As the result, they entangle over self-created problem for nothing. This is the real going on picfture in Nepalese societies and communities.

This book intends to put an end to people's over belief in gods and goddesses and their superstition to make them free from the suffering from evil spirits and all kinds of bad and black harmful spirits. In the book I have vividly placed four types of symbolic Mandalas in which seven tantrically meaningful letters are included in each Mandala . Some other new tantric appliances also presented in the book to draw people's special attention to it. I am sure if people follow all the rules and critarions mentioned in the book they will be able to be free from all kinds of evil spirits and harmful spirits. Again they will be quite capable to put away their belief in superstition and unnecessary over faith in gods and goddesses as well as their blind faith.

My main purpose of writing this book is to provide people

enough clear view about old religions and tantrism. I want to dash people for forwarding motion from chronic superstition to fresh reality so that they could handle their religious problem and black spirits. Also I want to draw attention of the people of other countries to make them know how people of Nepal are passing life in superstition sinking deeply in trouble on the one hand and role of tantrism to get relief for them from harmful elements on the other.

Along with the above purpose my another purpose of writing this book is to bring my new approach of tantrism in light to provide knowldge to the people of other countries about tantric healing in Nepal for the people who are suffering from evil spirits and all other kinds of harmful spirits. I hope I will be sucessful in this field to some extent.

A SHORT LOOK INTO CENTURY OLD TANTRISM

It is not a matter of wonder and doubt that tantrism is the practical aspect of religion that is as old as human being's stepping on the Earth. Cavemen when they used to suffer from Natural calamities such as earthquake, flood, unbearable heat and cold, Landslide etc. would pray with supreme or Almighty gods and goddesses to get them rid of such uncommon and unexpected Natural events. In those prehistoric time people, because of fear, would see supreme beings in the form of gods and goddesses everywhere in Air, in water, in fire, in the sky, on the land etc. would pray with them for their safety. Those supreme beings also would be pleased with people and would save them by using their uncommon power. This kind of uncommon high power used for actions religiously is tantrism. In all religions such aspect is found whether it is Hinduism or Buddhism or Christism or any other religions of the world.

Nepal, though a small country of the world in social, in economical, in political spheres is a religiously great country. People of this country have unsurpassable faith in gods and goddesses and they by performing different extraordinary religious activities had passed lot of time in worshipping and praying to please the Almighty gods and goddesses for their safety and for the protection of their country. They became able to please the Amities and got some super power for themselves. The power that they got as boon from gods and goddesses is used by them sometimes for themselves and sometimes for other people to help them or to hate them, to provide happiness for them or to hate them or to provide them pain and problem. In this way people used the practical power of divinely bestowed power upon them is called religion and its practice is tantrism.

Nepal, a beautiful small country of Asian continent, is abode of gods and goddesses. In this holy land here, it is a popular saying, 333 millions gods and goddesses are living with their different super power to be used to protect the people and the country, to make people free from all kinds of difficulties and problems that appear time to time on the way to lead life in a simple and easy motion. In every nook and corner of the country many gods and goddesses with many uncommon might and power are dwelling in various styled temples, monasteries watching all events of nature as phenomenons and event sent by evil spirits to create trouble in human life are checked to cause any major damage so that the innocent and sober people of Nepal should not weep because of misery, should not cry because of not being able to bear hardship on their shoulder. So in Nepal people are always happy and content due to unique mercy of supreme beings for lasting soft and sweet days in all years to come in the life of the people. At present, in Nepal about 24 millions people are breathing peacefully. Here number of gods and goddesses are many times more than the people. That's why people are quite safe and happy. Here is no any danger and harm internally and externally, for them. People have no fear of suffering at home and from abroad. Every stages of life of the people in Nepal is guarded by super being's multistrength. So in the country people being loyal devotees to gods and goddesses and spend their major part of time in pleasing the supermen or Lords. They worship them and offer them the things they have as fruits, food and flowers. They offer domesticated animals as goats, buffalos, ducks, cocks etc. to please supreme beings. From dawn to late night people read name of the gods and goddesses of power to get happiness and to gain salvation in life. People here adapt meditation to be away from all kinds of evil thinking, evil practices and black and selfish desire. They do meditation with hope of being great men in life by holding scented human services as seed of joy for all fellow beings according to their need.

Nepal is a land of multidimensional wonder. Here time to time wonder is created by human activities some are good and some are harmful activities that dash people to doubt, fear and uncertainty and they would be falling away from virtue, truth, honesty and firm determination rather would be moving here and there and everywhere with their own whim which throw ugly actions in many wings of family and society. Fear is the major factor which quakes mind of the people, which breaks sweet hope and leads them to downfall, dilapidated state and which forces people to surrender to super beings to get rid of such fear and uncertainty. It is fear that paves people's way to wind life to oscillation peacefully. People are ready to sacrifice their money and other things of values for salvation. Most of the people's time is spent in pleasing gods and goddesses without caring to go ahead showing the congenial and potential labour for concrete result. So they became idle and weak physically. Only just spelling greatly and highly name of various gods and goddesses they hope, lot in life as there is nothing worthy to count. Centuries passed but no change at all in the dealing and feeling of the people. No reforms in their actions and reactions, no rays in thinking and sinking to the very depth of reality, no appreciable motion in outlook and only clouds over human dwellings. Crimes and sins as the ugly product of fear were twinkling brightly above human weakness, narrowness, selfishness and voidness. People, because of lack of correct realisation to reach to destination, began to march to wrong way performing limitless worshipping, praying and asking for juiceless fruit and void thinking. But they thought they had got abstract success in life because of virtuous performance in religious infinite journey. But in faith, people could get nothing except, voidness. Every thing is given and spent but nothing is got and gained. This is the result of traditional religion that was originated as by-product of human fear.

In Nepal here are so many gods and goddesses that are very difficult to count. People here are always busy in religious performances to please those supreme beings with hope of happiness, prosperity and lasting success in life. But result of their such duty has been quite reverse for them. Some wicked persons want to do bad deeds. By praying, worshipping and offering things of great values to gods and goddesses they possessed evil power from those super beings. The boned evil power by supreme to them is used by them to other simple, social, honest and the best persons without due care and enjoyed much from human sufferings. Such evil minded persons, though they seem to be innocent outwardly are very hard, cruel and selfish inwardly. So they prevailed evil power around the country to drew many persons, into web of misery and difficulty. Use of such evil power of the wicked minded persons is supposed as unseen and non diagnosed diseases. It is a psychological and mental disease and could not be cured by the use of any popular medicines. When the evil or wicked minded persons apply their evil power no physician whether they belong to medical or surgical could not cure such invisible diseases at all. People when become victim of such wonderful diseases their nature and behaviour seem full of wonder. They sometimes weep sometimes laugh and cry without any clear reason. Those trouble givers are known as witch for female wizard for male persons. Their such action is known as witchcraft. In every nook and corner of the country since the time Immemorial such crafts were prevailing actively and continuously. Victims of such diseases have been wide spreading by covering majority of human doors. Such evil power of bad persons could be controlled and put away by the persons who had learnt all ways of this secret subject and also learnt method of pulling out by breaking the main root and shoot of it, persons who heal this unseen and complicated disease by using their magical medicines as spelled water, spelled ash and jantra prepared tantrically. Jantra, is a crystal medicine religiously prepared with secret ritual spell to use to the patients by the healer. It would be hung unseenly round the neck or to bind round the waist or bind it in a cross way from right to left or from left to right from shoulder to down up to waist. The spelled water is known as jal given by the healer to drink as liquid medicine and is used as directed by healer. It is advised by the healer to the patient to drink the spelled water (Jal) once or twice a day. Spelled ash which is known as Bibhuti. Healer advises the patients to use this spelled ash (Bihute) ritually prepared on their forehead. When the patient use this Bibhute they feel to be free from the misery of the disease. When the patients drink Jal (The spelled water) they feel to be free from pain in the body. When the patients use Jantra they build enough energy physically and get confidence in themselves that they will be cured soon from the disease. When jantra is used the patients could not be attacked by evil spirits and black spirits easily. So this thing is considered as a body guard to be safe from external attack whenever and wherever they move. So this spelled water (Jal), the spelled ash (Bibhuti) and jantra (the crystled medicine to guard the body) are panacea which are quite fit to all kinds of unseen diseases caused by evil spirits or evil persons. The persons who handle such wonderful and fearful disease is known by different names in different communities. They are known as Jhakray, Vaidhya, Prabhu, Guru, Dhami, Thakali etc. In every community such persons can be found and according to need of the people they would be serving them to get rid of miseries. People give them something gift as money, cloth, other valuable things etc. The witchcraft is found more in number in the undeveloped, underdeveloped and developing countries. Specially it is found in the rural area of the country because majority of people there are illiterate and believe in superstition. So the elder and the eldest person of the community as people believe them and think that they have divine power to check and control the evil spirits. People go to them with their grievances to be free from such mysterious disease and ask Thakali, Prabhu, Jhakry, Dhami, Vaidhya, priest for necessary action to heal their disease through tantric doctrine. All things required for healing will be fulfilled by the patients or patients family. Everywhere the heals are respected and honoured by the people for their holy service.

Those healers not only check, or put away the witches and wizards they could put away other all kinds of evil spirits. Ghosts and many other kinds of phantom like evil spirits are other agent that easily bring uneasy disturbance in human life.

Evil spirits regularly visiting in a place and occasionally in other places snatch human peace and happiness. Such kinds of evil spirits also could be put away by healers Thakali, Jhakray, Prabhu, Priest, monks, sages, Dhami etc. by performing religious performances. But the healers could not fix time for making people free them from evil spirits. They can make free sometimes in very short time and sometimes it takes long time. It depends upon nature of disease and pouring of tantric spell on and in the evil spirits. Effective pouring of the effective tantric spell to put away pain and problem of the patients though abstract in colour and nature can produce quite practical impact to make the patients free if the time factor, application of secret spell and correct or proper channel to flow magic or tantric power of the healer are quite intact.

Tantrism is the practical aspect of the religion. Every religion has possessed such tantric quality more or less as one of its wings. By applying this quality those persons who have gained sound experience in this field can show wonderful display by curing unseen, unknown and mysterious disease which are totally complex in symptom are psycho mental diseases are very difficult to find out their main root. The witch craft is deep rooted in the social soil though not measured exactly and seriously has grown up with various branches of different shapes and sizes and has been a very hard mental anxiety and has devoured peace of mind slowly and silently. In the vast religious ocean of humanity the evil spirits' swimming and flying here and there damaged the human heart as in the natural oceans the poisonous snakes, crocodiles and sea monsters have created horror and damaged the human heart and other watery simple and quite creatures. Religion is totality of good moral rules and regulations put in practice by the people to deal with evil spirits and black spirits. So since ancient time people have put these codes of conduct to be free from such bad living elements. William Shakespeare in most of his dramas has entertained such evil spirits in various ways with a view to make people familiar with them and to make people careful from such spirits. Some scenes of the witches and ghosts and other peculiar spirits in his dramas are vivid examples to know how the great dramatist tried to make people attentive of such elements. As recorded in Greek mythology and in the myths of other countries where there are vivid social and historical events highly coloured by religion it is easy to find the mentioned harmful role played by evil spirits that negatively influenced the human life to drag it to pain and anxiety to change strength into weakness to make life as void and useless. Similar and more miraculous than that or same type of acts of evil spirits are recorded in Nepal in the form of myth, in the form of social events and in the form of historical as well as religious record. So I have tried to pour down all major events of this land one by one to make other people understand how those evil spirits and black spirits have danced on the social stage of Nepal and how they destroyed peace of human dwellings. As Nepal is home of gods and goddesses here every where evil spirits and black spirits also are living getting grace of the supremes. But their living has been hidden and unknown to common flocks. Such spirits raise their head to create miseries in human dwellings by spreading black magical spells. Here in Nepal many historical silent records are maintained to prove the existence of such hateful and fearful beings. Witches and wizards are outwardly normal living beings as other normal human beings. But they have learnt the witchcraft by following all conditions and doctrines given by their preacher. In fact, to learn this kind of secret craft female persons had to perform special religious worshipping, meditation and praying to gods and goddesses to get blessing for their wished secret action. It is said to be perfect in this black craft the learners whether they are male or female must offer their most valuable thing. Female learners had to alter their husband or child to god and goddess. So most of the female persons who had learnt this secret witchcraft had been seen as widows or losers of children. Again they must always at any time be ready to give the thing to their preachers when they are asked otherwise the preacher would be angry with them and could be accused of their inability. But whatever the way and doctrine to get this ugly craft may be it has been great problem, a century old social problem passing from one generation to another generation. So people of generations on way highly or mildly were and are suffering from this black and evil craft. People, even in this modern time of science and technology are being victim to this ugly and unseen diseases caused by this harmful craft. In Nepal majority of people are poor illiterate, innocent. They had belief in witchcraft and are suffering much. Those Jhakray, Dhami, Guru, Prabhu, Vaidhya, Shadhu, monks, etc. are here in many number and are ready, to help those sufferers to make them free from such peculiar suffering. This kind of unseen and unknown mysterious diseases are still here in the country. It is so deep rooted in every nook and corner of the country that it can't be rooted out completely for ever. This disease falls on human body in any time as simple disease as fever or any other serious disease that makes its way in any body and causes shaking in the body in a peculiar and unexpected way sometimes mildly and sometimes hardly.

The witchcraft is a wonderful craft which has very high power of flight. Witches/wizards who have thoroughly learnt this craft can fly their soul or spirit thousands of miles away from their dwelling or can fly to the person to whom they had intended to touch. They can change their form according to their need. They sometimes become cats sometimes become dogs or any other in the form of cat, dog or rat. They, there and then, enter in human body and show various stages of their ruling over the human body by making change in appearance, by speaking in totally different in tune by sudden high laughing, by weeping bitterly, by shouting horribly etc. The witches or wizards entering in other's body can't be known by other ordinary persons. Until the person who has such evil spirit in his/her body shows different sign and symptoms. In fact, witchcraft is a chain of many events that always creates pain, anxiety, unbearable problems that can't be described early. This much only can be said that witchcraft is century old craft of Nepal and is still existing here in the same force.

Another evil spirit that appears time to time in human houses of Nepal is ghost and creates horror in the mind of the people. What is a ghost? Why and how it appears in human houses? People have their own opinion. Religion has divided human life into two parts one is outward part that is body and another part is inward part that is soul. Body dies but soul does not die. In time of death of the man soul that is invisible comes out of body with last breath of life. It takes round within the four walls of the house. When it gets a comfortable place that is a small hole on the wall or ceiling or any others places of the house it hides and stays there for long time. It time to time comes out of the hole and takes round the house as phantom. Specially at night it appears as real figure of the dead person and creates horror in the mind of the concerned persons. Mostly ghosts appear at home on the occasion of feasts and festivals. Those days are religiously considered as special days, hard days and great days. In such days ghost in a form of phantom of dead children are seen by parents and ghosts of parents are seen by son and daughter of dead persons. The ghosts of parents, children, dead persons appear in the house when special provision of food prepared in feasts and festivals is not kept aside for them in a traditional way. Another reason of appearing ghosts at home is when ritual functions in their name is done in wrong way or not done forgetting them they do not be happy in such cases and appear in the house. Again another cause of appearing the ghosts is because of unnatural death of the persons. It a man or woman is killed or hung unnaturally against his/her will he/she time to time, appears at home and creates problem for family members. The ghosts create pain and problems mentally and physically until their soul is not pacified. If a man or woman sees a ghost all of sudden and he or she is weak and becomes sick because of the horror caused by the ghost. If he/ she is strong and his/her heart has enough power to resist such problem nothing will happen for him or her. But in general sense the ghosts are evil spirits. So they are things to disturb human mind by spreading fear in the living beings, dwelling. If the ghosts regularly appear in the houses of the people they fall in great horror and later there will be mental disease in them. So this evil spirit, the ghost should be put an end to as soon as possible to maintain constant mental peace in the family environments. But such trouble created by the ghosts can be rooted out. By the people by performing holy religious activities such as 'Hom' a relief action done religiously to put this evil spirit out of sight and out of mind of the people. It is a record that more numbers of males and females suffer from the ghosts. Such spirits haunts much to weak, persons physically and mentally. So mostly children and females suffer much. If people believe it they manage to be free from it but those who do not believe may suffer much from it not knowing the proper solution to save themselves. This ghost problem is not a problem of a particular person, place or of country. It is more of less a problem of the people of most of the parts of the world. Because of science and technology in use in the world people are courageous and practical minded and became away from blind belief and traditional religion. As the result, the high influence of the ghost has been not so effective. But here is still such evil and black spirits in the world they have played a high role to influence upon human beings.

The people see time to time in their life is another black and evil spirit. That is known as khyak. This khayak is seen in the human dwelling at late night time. About this spirit people of Nepal have talked much and have described about it in the my theological and religious books. This abstract, wonderful and fearful super spirit appear in the dark place and it's body structure is completely black with bright eyes. It often comes in human door not only to make people surprise but it also creates horror in the mind of the people. When there is lonely darkness in the house that is the favourable time for khyak to move here and there. It appears at home and sometimes it appears in the land too when there is quite calm at night. But this spirit sometimes becomes harmful and some times it becomes useful for human beings. It is said that it sometimes helps people for material gain. People say that there are white khyaks. This white one never cause any harm to people. When such khyak enters in the house automatically the house will be prosperous. Such khyak is very rare and can't be seen easily and often by the people as they see black khyaks. Only virtuous persons see or meet such white khyak. Normal khyaks are black from head to foot. They can be found or seen in any moment in the dark place. Such black spirits (khyaks) are more harmful but occasionally less useful. When weak persons and children see such black spirit in darkness they become sick because of high fear in them. If anybody want to see the shape and size, appearance and colours of khyak they can see its painted or copied figure on the wall of the temples, Dharmasala (religious inn constructed as charity lodge for priests, shadus and monks and travellers). Mock khyak can be seen in local religious cultural dance of Mahakali dance of Nepal. Though these spirits are not so harmful like other evil spirits people are afraid of them and pray to god not to send such spirit in their house in darkness. As khyak is a black spirit it always likes to stay or live in dark place and appears in the dark night. But at present such black spirits are going to vanish in human residential area due to lack of gloominess. Every house, every road and every lane of urban area is electrified and those places became quite unfit for this black spirit to roam here and there and it moved somewhere away from town. But even to these days khyaks are existing in rural area of Nepal.

Another evil being that is mentioned in the history of Hindu religion is a female evil spirit. It is known as kitchkani. This evil spirit also time to time can be seen by the people in their residential area. This evil spirit also appears at night with a view to hypnotize people and lead them to death or alter. As this is a female evil spirit it can hypnotize young persons by attracting to its high beauty and ripe youth. In late night to the dark lonely places by the human residence kitchkani often appears standing in a pathetic way showing young womanly beauty and youth to attract the young persons It seems as if she was denounced by her family. When young person would come across with such spirit he falls in her web being in blind passion and would be ready to enjoy with her thinking that it is an golden opportunity given by chance. Persons would loose their temper and sense when they see this beautiful kitchkani and follow her being just like a dumb driven cattle. As a result, this evil spirit by captivating young persons lead to alter. There will be the end of life. So this is very dangerous evil spirit than other black and evil spirits. In fact, kitchkani is evil being, seems quite polite, full of youth with praisable beauty. So young persons become victim to this spirit easily and lose their life. But clever persons can get rid of the web of this spirit by looking at her feet. The feet of such evil spirit have been opposite to ordinary persons. Feet are turned back. This is the only sign to know that it is evil spirit that devour human life. So people of ancient time never stay out at night. Such mysterious women standing in the junction of the road, by the side of temple and inn and never show any sympathy to them when they see such extraordinary life in the darkness of night of the solitary place. But such spirit can't be seen in the lighted place and the day time.

Kankal (kawoncha) is also an evil spirit available in Nepal. It can damage human peace and harmony by creating unnatural horror and fear in human beings dwellings. This evil spirit has peculiar formation. It is a spirit without flesh, blood and skin. The only found thing in such spirit is bone. So it is just like a skeleton. It also moves here and there in late night and midnight. It is a terrible spirit with harmful moves. Its peculiar horrorful crying is assumption of its arrival in human residence that indicates bad time for human beings. It's crying is a long crying just like jackle's crying. When anybody hear the crying of the kankal persons will be ill. So it is said that the heart thrilling crying of kankal is sign of going away of human happiness and coming of heavy rain of misery. So people perform religious work to please gods and goddesses to check such evil spirits' coming in the residential areas. Human beings can't do any thing against such evil spirit except bearing bad days if supreme power of gods do not prevent this evil spirit.

Bhauta is another evil creature that dwells in an unknown place but comes in human dwelling off and on and causes great harm for human beings. It is an abstract giant like evil creature that destroys human happiness and peace by consuming all stored food. It is belief of the people that this evil spirit brings famine by consuming all food required for human beings. People think this evil spirit brings famine by consuming all food required for human beings. People die in starvation if this evil creature appears time to time in human residence. So people offer some food to this spirit to please it when it visits in their dwelling. People never forget to set some food for this spirit in time of feast and festival to turn them back to its unknown place by satisfying it. But it is a very difficult task for the people to please the Bhuta because little quantity of food is not enough for it. It takes much food and never be food enough. People are afraid of this spirit for its appearance is full of horror. The favourable time for Bhuta to come to human dwelling is night time. The atmosphere suitable for it is quite and calm time of late night or midnight to roam around the human residence. People who saw this evil spirit say that it is a tall black phantom that at any time can be out of human sight. In different time it comes with different view in different shape and size. So it is very difficult to narrate such evil spirit in correct way one's saying about this evil spirit is quite different from another's saying. It is so because of multi shape and size of this creature. This evil spirit creates trouble to the people by dashing them to voidness or shortage of things. Bhuta lage chha' this is a popular saying of the people of Nepal. The meaning of the saying is the evil spirit Bhuta has entered in the house or in the body of the person. When such evil spirit enters in the house no body could be satisfied in the house there will be food problem until this spirit leaves the house. If a person is dominated by this evil element he/she consumes much more food yet he/she would not be satisfied. Such person always seems to be hungry and thirsty. So people are always careful to close the door of their house to prevent entering Bhuta in their house. So wise and careful person in Nepal look back to know if they are followed by such harmful spirit.

Preta is another evil spirit is not lesser than other evil spirits and black spirits to bring bad and trouble situation in people's life. It gives lot of unbearable pain and anxiety in the life. It gives lot of unbearable pain and anxiety in the life of the people in one or other way to put them on the horns of dilemma. It sucks human blood. When this Preta spirit raises its head in human being's land it thwarts people's desire and always provides them pungent things that they could not digest at all for health and that they could not like to taste to be in upset condition mentally and physically. About this evil spirit also people of different view have expressed their view differently.

Some say that it is the product of unnatural death. When persons die unwillingly or when persons die accidentally without fulfilling any even their minor desire in this case their soul will be disturbed and it will not move away from the dwelling place. So soul of such persons appears here and there in the residence time to time and creates horror for living persons. As the result, it makes persons thrilling and shaking when they see the terrible sight. It also can early weaken persons mentally and physically. So person may be ill by seeing such harmful spirit. For the recovery of health of sick persons magic spell of tantric healing is fit instead of medicine.

These all evil spirits and black harmful spirits mentioned above were great super and extra ordinary spirits for the people of ancient time. In those by gone days and nights people instead of suffering from different diseases they would suffer much form merciless attack of those bad and harmful evil spirits and black spirits. So in those days of ancient time people would rush to healers. Those healers were vaidhya, Jhakre, Dhami, monks, sages, Prabhu, Thakali, priests etc. Those healers by spelling the ritual tantric spell infuse their powerful spell over the patients and make them quite will and by taking them away from the clutch of the evil spirits and black spirts. The patients would be free from pain and problems caused by those spirits. But all methods of tantric healing for various diseases used by the healers are based upon secret religions ritual spell of high power. This tantrism is the practical branch or side of the religions to be applied for medical cure which is known as tantric healing. To make persons more clear about such evil spirits and black spirits that belong to religion as its active part that causes great damage in human settlement on and on, I have presented profiles of some of the major powerful evil spirits and black spirits. Those are as following in the picture.

(a) Witch *(b)* wizard *(c)* khyak *(d)* ghost *(e)* Kitchkani *(f)* Bhuta *(g)* Preta *(h)* Kankal (kawancha).

The evil spirits shown in the picture are major spirits of trouble and problem creators. They time to time create trouble in human life to snatch away peace, prosperity happiness and success of human beings to turn them to critical and dilapidated

Different Kinds of evil and black spirits

condition. Persons whoever they may be rich or poor, soft natured or hard natured, cruel or kind etc. can be victim to such spirits as a religious curse in life. But persons suffering from such mysterious and wonderful trouble and problem can be free after having complete course of treatment from religious experts or tantric headers. Thank god for their unique and holy service to human beings to bring back the people to their normal state in life.

In fact, those all trouble creating evil spirits are by-product of century old traditional religions. As the religion based on fear it produced doubts and confusion in human mind. People became very far from certainty and sanity. Truth and self confidence lost in mist. People of simple and gentle nature fell on the horns of dilemma by not knowing the path of reality. They lost the way of light and doctrine of happy life on the Earth. Because of superstition, misguidance, immature vision, firm determination majority of people in Nepal fell in black deeds of evil spirits and suffered much repented much getting worries much. Still now people are moving every where with hope of being free from the attack of such evil black and bad spirits. Suffering caused by evil spirits has been of the same type and same effect are mostly treated as mental disease that can't be treated and checked by using popular medical apparatus and wildly used medicines as directed by the physicians.

There are totally different methods and medicines which are very simple and available in all human doors. Generally the popular medicines for such sufferings caused by such harmful spirits are *(a)* The ritually spelled water to be used to drink by the patient and *(b)* the ritually spelled ash prepared to be used on the forehead of the patient. These both holy things should be used for several days by patient as he is directed. All methods or doctrines directed to him/her to do should be done strictly. Again in some major cases some extra things also should be used or should be done to heal the disease quickly. In the name of gods and goddesses of power religious performance should be done to please those supremes. To please those supremes. The religious performance should be done in different ways, in different place and in different time. Some religious performance should be done for few hours but some will take days and weeks. Choice of place for the religious performance also differs. Some will be by the side of the grave and again some will be in the high land by the side or under the Bar and Pipal trees. Time favourable for such holy performances is the morning and night time. But quite favourable time for major diseases is Late night to midnight. Again favourable days to put away or to control the evil spirits and black spirits by applying holy ritual performances are Saturday and Tuesday. These two days are quite suitable days for evil spirits and black spirits to perform their harmful action. In these two days these harmful and hateful spirits appear at home and in any other places. These two days Saturday and Tuesday are the best days for the healers too to hold remedial steps to check or control such harmful spirits by performing powerful ritual action. But raw force and power of the human being is nothing to overcome the evil spirits attack on them. People must be favoured by gods and goddesses of power to put an end to the miseries and troubles caused by bad black and unnatural evil beings. Without the favour of gods and goddesses power nobody can remove the pain and problems of those evil spirits and black spirits. The healers became healers for they pleased the gods and goddesses of power to get enough power-the super power of divine, being in the strict rules of religion to preform all the stages of required ritual acts. As they succeeded to possess such divine power they applied it over those trouble creating spirits and became able to get victory over those bad and evil spirits. Those healers as priests, Jhakrays, Dhamis Vaidhyas, monks, sages, Shadhus, Thakalies etc. all went through the ritual process to get the divine power of gods and goddesses of power and became capable to put away and control all kinds of evil spirits and black spirits.

As Nepal is abode of gods and goddess people here are always protected by Almighty gods and goddesses. When here appears any uncommon events caused by Nature or it is caused by evil or black spirits people would not be afraid of such events. They go to temples and monasteries and perform ritual performance. They offer all things that make supreme powers please to help them to be free from all unhappy days. They all perform ritual performances. When Almighty uses super power in favour of people of Nepal those evil spirits will be away from all places of human reach and there will be peace and harmony in all human beings residence. Witches, wizards also create unbearable trouble and misery to the people to quench their inhuman thirsty they use their power given by gods and goddesses to do such evil or harmful acts. But in the long run the supremes will be angry with such harmful persons for their harmful work they will be punished by gods in the misuse of power for their selfish motive. Almighty gods and goddess are always in favour of justice and truth and always look after good persons who are simple, honest and devoted to Almighty. So Almighty by sending many kinds of thundering and lighting enough to pains and problems punishes witches and wizards and protect all human beings from the heavy rain of misfortune. But in case of other super evil and black spirits as khyak, Ghost, Kitchkani, Bhuta, Preta, Kankal etc. people can get rid of them only by pleasing Almighty gods and goddesses. So people worship gods and goddesses when they fall in the pain and problem caused by any one of those super evil beings and black beings. As in science in religion also has many Mantras or rules of moral conduct to be followed by human beings to please, to honour and to worship gods and goddesses to grow all kinds of success and joy of life. The divine codes of conduct are made by representatives of the gods and goddesses of power according to the divine will. Here representatives mean priests, sages, monks Jews etc., who, it is said, have direct link with supreme power. Almighty gods and goddesses have ruled over the universe. So in the realm of religion virtue is the victor vice is the victim. Human will be winner and evil spirits and black spirits will be losers. This is the common and popular belief of the people since the time immemorial till this brave modern world.

Now here is brief narration about gods and goddesses of power and their unique high unavoidable command like rule to use them in people's life and about how they would make people free from all sorts of pain and problems poured in life by evil spirits and black spirits. According to the religion followed by people as their duty from the very beginning of human beings living on the Earth and how gods and goddesses of different power are treated, looked and regarded by the people should be known clearly to understand the role of religion and the significance of it in human life of then and now also to be evaluated very sincerely to measure tantric weight of the religion which is considered as practical religion to cure the people when they suffer from unknown and undiagnosed diseases. I have intended to narrate the synopsis of two antagonistic religious evil force and human welfare force. Evil force is the force of evil spirits and black spirits whereas the human welfare is force of Sages, monks, Dhami, Jhakre, priests etc. In fact, the religion is the combination of these two forces.

Hindu religion is old, mysterious, liberal and full of virtue. It has many ways of religion. People have to come across with many kinds of formula and useful super beings and extra ordinary beings. Angels, faries, deities etc. are good super beings that always bestow good things upon human beings for their happy life. Witches/wizards, ghosts, Bhauta-Preta, Pesacha etc. are evil spirits. That always' push people to trouble, pain, problem and misery. It is all known and all accepted fact that religion began form human fear. In ancient time in the stone Age men were passing a very humble life. They did not know what is happiness of men. They had very hard life and was very difficult to lead ever a simple hands to month life. They had problems borne in every step of life internally and externally. As men of the stone Age had to live in the cave with fear in their mind they were very uncertain to their life. Their main roots of fear were fear of Earthquake, fear of landslide, flood and famine. Other minor fear were attack of wild animals and attack from other group of men. Because of various fear externally people saw every where in the sky, in the water, on the land different kinds of images of various shapes and sizes of peculiar power, dealing and feeling people time to time found some of those images seemed angry with them and some of them seemed happy with them. Again people found some of those images seemed quite serious and grave to them. So they were afraid of those imaginary images. They supposed those all kinds of imaginary images were super beings. They thought those all were gods and goddesses. People began to please those images of the sky, the land and water and also began to worship and offer them things to gain favour from those supremes. This people's religious performance continued for ever and it is regarded as faith paving and relief providing essential elements for human protection and preservation of humanity or human solidarity. On this background Hindu religion is originated and put in practice for happiness. As time passed on here appeared many gods and goddesses in this religion. All gods and goddesses have super power which is applied for benefit of the people and such power is used to finish the evil spirits and black spirits. So people placed the supreme gods and goddesses in their houses and in the temples with high respect and honour thinking that they are guards of people, fate makers and mercy providers. Thousands and thousands of gods and goddesses with various power and capacity appeared to the people in their praying. Different gods and goddesses are named differently according to the types of their help to the people. People prayed those supreme Lords to fulfil their desire and to get relief. From that time people began to pass most of the time in worshipping and praying to Lords. Many Almighty gods and goddesses are found in every nook and corner in the holy realm of religion. In this way, Hindu religion was passing years, decades and centuries. Devotion and meditation are two wings of Hindu religion. These two wings cover complete religious activities such as Homs and Yagyas. So according to this religion devotion and meditation are the ways to salvation in the life of the people. Those who are devotees to lords or supreme gods and goddesses perform ritual performances sincerely following all religions doctrines are happy and successful persons. They get to enter in the heaven to pass their life happily in the unknown place with all heavenly things to enjoy. Being in great hope people since the ancient time have been busy by heart and soul in devotion and meditation to gain known and unknown joy in life here and away from here. But for me these kinds of religious activities and ritual performances are completely abstract and mysterious can't be advantageous to gain any solid thing in human life. Devotion and meditation though they are beneficial personally it leads people to voidness, idleness, weakness, uncertainty, backward, parasite nature and behaviour etc. which are poison-like qualities to take people to development and straight forwardness to strengthen for themselves, their coming generation and their country. But it does not mean that religion misshapes the humanity, it does not mean religion is antagonistic thing to spiritualism. My only saying to the people of Hindu religion is they must use the religion very carefully by limiting it as pure and holy one to purify their mind to maintain lasting peace and harmony in human life. Major part of human life should be used quite actively and full of energetic motion to gain material requirement to pass daily life easily and comfortably amid the abundance. So religion should be used as a key to alround development physically to fulfil all material quench in a sane or pure way and spiritually perfect to maintain peace and honesty in any condition in the life of persons. In fact, religion is an abstract, holy and virtuous linkage between human beings and super human beings, between lords and men and between heavenly beings and Earthly beings to set up perennial close link for security of human beings for mitigating all sin, inhuman activities, and natural calamities. But in going on Hindu religion there is lack of potentiality to build up human personality, to achieve physical fitness to ensure all necessary things of life. As the religion is deductive in nature it grows and ripen only in faithful mind of the religions persons. No question, no doubt, no argument is permitted to reach to reason. Organs of body are moved slowly and lightly to clap hands, to turn head to look at gods and goddesses, to move legs to go to home of the super beings. Such style of men do not help them to be hopeful for progress. So to make human fate bright in the lights of smooth development there must be balance between religious beauty and human duty. Hindu religion though is considered as the older religion, is sentimental than practical is dogmatic than to be effective reality and is orthodoxical data processing concept than high potential virtue.

Religion is quite rigid. Such quality is its defect. There should be possibility of change in religion to harmonise it with change of time, taste of people and faith of the people. Again there is lack of flexibility in religion. So, people put it a little away form them. They began to count religion as volunteering thing and optional subject to be used as scent to draw other's attention as men of sanity, going to home of gods and goddesses has been a fashion to hide crime form the public. Any theology can't be fit for all time and for all people to come. So there should be reformative possibility in the religion to make it countable as effective one. Now to stop this flow of my view here I have crossed the road to narrate other side of the religion of Hindu kingdom Nepal to high light action oriented power of gods and goddesses which is known as tantrism.

Most of the gods and goddesses of Hindu religion have their own super power operative to create astonishment in the people so that the people can be put in control and can't be moved with courage of opposing them. Gods and goddesses have both good and bad power to be applied for human beings. So all super beings or Lords of the universe that rule over all human beings are supremely superior and no normal people can match them in any respect of life though they venture to plan against them. In the vast realm of Hindu religion the gods of power are mainly god Shiva is also known as lord Mahadeva, Lord krishna, god Ganesh, god Bhairab, god Brahma, god Vishnu, god Indra, Lord Ram, god Hanuman, god Mahakali Lord Kumar etc. Among the goddesses main goddesses are goddess Durga Bhawani known as Bhagabati, goddess Saraswoti, goddess Laxmi, goddess Parbati, goddess Kali, Goddess Sita, goddess Radha etc. are goddesses of power. Their power is multi dimensional with two blades. One is good power time to time is used over human beings to reward and to punish the people for their virtue and vice. When there will be injustice, crime, malpractices, suppression and unnatural sufferings and miseries over people by people at such time super beings of power use their power to protect good people. When there will be mischievous work, and evil work done by bad persons against gods and goddesses or good and simple people in this case bad power will be prevailed over them to punish. All those gods and goddesses of power perform their duty or power according to need of the people. Gods of power as Lord Shiva, Lord Krishna, Lord Indra, Lord Brahma, Lord Ganesh, Lord Bhairab Lord Vishnu etc. who have supreme power show their peculiar tantric wonder in any moment in the human dwelling positively and negatively. The appearance and disappearance of gods of power in any form as they like is full of wonder, full of delight and full of horror etc. By applying the tantric power those gods and goddesses can flow any thing water, milk, blood etc. abundantly, can change brightness into gloominess, can cause no raining or heavy raining and do many other miraculous deeds as they like to do in all human dwellings. It is mentioned in the religion that everything is possible for those Lords of power and they can display their super actions in any time in any part of the world. People can't oppose the gods' and goddesses' actions rather they have to watch all wonderful film of super beings goings on before their eyes as boon or gift for them from them. People have to say this much that their rise and fall, happiness and misery, success and failure, abundance and scarcity etc. are god's and goddess's mercy, protection and supervision, Nobody venture to go against god's will if goes he/she will suffer much unbearably in the life. As evil spirits and black spirits as witch/wizards, Bhuta, Preta, Khyak, Kankal which are considered as by-products of the religion to cause trouble, fear, problems etc. on human beings try to draw people to them. But people having blessing of super beings gods and goddesses of power can be safe from the attack of any evil elements and black elements. People are free form the evil spirits by getting mercy of gods and goddesses. They are fortune makers of the people. So people put Almighty gods and goddesses in human residential land by placing them in high position in the temple and monastery. The abodes of gods and goddesses have unique style. Abodes or temples differ slightly or vastly in the shape and size, height, length and breath each other. Now let me here demonstrate pictures of some well known temples of supreme Lords of power. Temples and monasteries are abodes of gods and goddesses are holy places where people crowd every day with hope of salvation, peace of mind, meditation to be free from problems, fear, tears, doubts sin and various black and evil deeds. People visit to temples and monasteries with hope of development of human unity with sweet welfare for ever safety from all kinds of natural calamities. Again people visit in the abodes of Almighty lords for praying, worshipping, getting bless, taking part in religious hymns. Hindu religion says that homes of gods and goddesses are only centres where people go to submit their life to supreme lords when they will be helpless and hopeless, when they could not bear human troubles and miseries and when they could not find peace and happiness in any human dwellings. Temples are the place of inspiration, purification, truth and beauty, so people feel quite content in the supremes dwellings. So people whoever and wherever they may be eager to visit in more homes of the gods and goddesses before stepping to the grave hoping that they would be able to enter in the heaven after leaving this Earth. But, at present, because of changes brought by time people have adopted religion lightly and many misunderstanding and misinterpretations are being taken place in this realm. As the result, devotees time to time fell under the clouds of confusion and often began to walk randomly without any concrete religious aim. So they became far from virtue, religious beauty and religious sweet scent. But now visiting to temples has been a religious fashion and has no religious value in it. As religion is older than science and other social and political subjects it is still deep rooted in the mind of the people. So they could not still venture to deny its lessons and instructions though they are void and not substantial thing for them. People's belief for happiness, peace and prosperity in them is big and vast. So the religious tree is still growing up higher and higher and people are eager to pluck pure and fresh fruit in it to lead sweet and soft life on the Earth. It is said by dignified sages, priests and hermits of Hindu religion that it is very old and great religion and it has many branches. Each branch has abundant fruits of knowledge useful to pass life successfully on the soil being men of salt for solid achievement. But due to lack of proper direction & instruction, due to misguidance and misinterpretation of religious lessons and principles and due to anti religious view of the great religious teachers and preachers of the religion the potentiality of this popular religion has been faded away in every succeeding year in the world. It is so because religion is rigid subject that has adopted unchangeable morality totally coloured in pure moral codes. Time changed mind of the people and every thing of the world changed. But Hindu religion does not change at all. This quality of the religion is its drawback that caused people to be away silently. So light of this religion has been dim to see the reality or growth of inspiration. Religion of Hindus consist many abstracts full of mysterious and amazing moral codes that can't be described in few limited pages. So in my this writing I have focused my attention to narrate only gods and goddesses of immense power of tantrism which in every step of human life has been hard to speculate whether that is good or bad for the people. In fact, tantric displays of the supreme Lords are practical aspect of the religion. Such action is religious magic to turn fate of the people from well to good, from rise to fall, from owe to well and fall to rise. In the counting Lords or gods of power firstly I pronounce Lords or gods of power. I pronounce Lord Mahadeva. Mahadeva is greatly eminent god of tantric power of Hindu religion.

Lord Maha-Deva :—Lord Maha Deva is the great god of Hindu religion. This lord is the symbol of multidimensional super power. Lord Mahadeva is also known as Lord Shiva is the god of human welfare and benevolence. For peace and happiness in human dwellings Lord Shiva used his unique super power to check evil spirits and black spirits. Disguising as sage and various ordinary beings, Lord Mahadeva visits everywhere to get rid of human beings hard troubles and problems. In the praying of the persons spelling as 'Har Har Maha Deva' Lord Maha Deva used his amazing power and would send heavy rain fall to flow water every where in people's residence. 'Jaya sambhu' this is another addressing to Lord Maha deva by the devotees. In time of smoking 'gaanja' people spell great words 'Jaya Sankar'. It is well known fact to the people of Hindu religion that Maha deva is highly fond of 'gaanja'. Lord Maha Deva always stands for justice in human life and always put evil spirits away from human beings by using his high power. And always provides all essential things of virtue for the people. So Lord Shiva spreads his tantric power here, there and every where for the betterment of human beings to maintain peace and harmony in their dwelling. Lord Maha Deva is the great divine dancer. He used to play trick to put an end to evil spirits and other harmful spirits by captivating them in his wonderful dance. He ended Bhasmasur captivating in his super dance. Snake is lord Maha Deva's favourite pet that always remains round his neck as garland. In fact, the snake functions as sincere guard of Lord Shiva. The High snowy mountain known as Kailash is his favourite residence. He lives there with his spouse goddess Parbati. Lord Maha deva's tantric power is so great and powerful that it is beyond description. No evil and devil spirits resist in the use of his such high power.

As Nepal is Hindu kingdom and the favourite residence of Mahadeva also belongs to Nepal. Here every year a great national religious festive day is celebrated to pay tribute to Lord Maha deva. This special religious day is known to all people of the country as Maha Shiva Ratri. On the eve of this holyday great religious performance, religious song of praying known as Bhajan would be celebrated in every nook and corner of Nepal. The mammoth crowd of devotees of the country and from the abroad gather around the temple of Lord Shiva in Pashupati, a holy place for pilgrim of Hindus on the auspicious occasion. From neighbouring countries specially from India many devotees visit in Pashupati Nath temple on this holy occasion. Praying, worshipping, religious singing, religious dancing meditation etc. would be performed enthusiastically. Here, in Nepal, is National holiday on the eve of this religious great day. It has been a custom to include this praying from the Head of the state 'May Lord Pashupati Nath save the country and the people' in every royal proclamation. This is the short narration of tantric god Lord Maha Deva to make people clear how Maha Deva is regarded by the people of Nepal.

Lord Krishna :—Lord Krishna is another supreme god of high power in Hindu religion. People believe that god krishna

Abodes or Temples of Gods and goddesses

Krishna Temple, Patan, Nepal

Backside of Pashupati Nath

Taleju Temple, Kathmandu, Nepal

Nyata Pol Temple, Bhaktapur, Nepal

Hindu Temples, Kath of Hanuman Dhoka, Durbar

Mahaboudha Tempal of Patan, Nepal

SWAYAMBHUNATH STUPA
KATHMANDU

Ram-Janaki Temple of Janakpur, Nepal

Mukti Nath Temple, Nepal

always uses his supreme power in different style for the welfare of human beings to save them from all sorts of evil, hard and dark problems. Lord krishan, it is said, takes great anxiety when there appears unnatural events in human dwellings. In such cases he in the guise of different ordinary and simple being visits to human residential areas to check up the ugly harmful events for perennial flow of peace and happiness in all parts of human reaches (residences). If any kinds of evil and black spirits or devils become a problem for the people Lord krishna uses his high power in favour of truth and destroys devil and evil spirits. Hindu religion mentions it to highlight the supreme high power of Lord Krishna that it is Lord krishna who poured unmatchable power in 'The Mahabharat' in favour of Pandav as a symbol of truth and backed Pandavs to reach to winning pole in the great war between Kaurav and Pandav, a war between virtue and vice. Like Maha Deva Lord Krishna also is god of Bishowroop that means he can take any guise according to the need of time. Lute is the favourite musical instrument of Lord Krishna. He can influence highly upon gopineens (maids) by playing it in a magical style. As Lord Krishna is the god of high power of human benevolence he always watches, keenly the going on pictures in human dwellings and apply power for the betterment of mankind by putting all dangers and harms to the end. There is a religious book known as 'Geeta' in which many moral codes like preachings of Lord krishna are found in verse. All Hindus follow these moral preachings of lord Krishna for truth and moral beauty in human life. Hermits, monks, sages of Hindu religion have studied 'Geeta' and digested it thoroughly. They preach general people the religious codes or laws of Hindu religion and Lord krishna's divine philosophy mentioned in the Geeta to make people reform all bad and harmful behaviour and manner, thinking etc. to pass life properly, prosperously in peace and happiness.

Lord Ram—is another great god of ideal, tolerance, truth and beauty of Hindu religion. Power of obedience to senior is another special remark of Lord Ram. He preaches devotees that they have to face problems and miseries with patience and tolerance to step to the way to success. Victory is the product of sacrifice is sweet religious lesson to people from Lord Ram to encourage the devotees to be ready to give up even valuable things for the victory of truth in life. Victory of Lord Ram over demon monarch Ravan of Lanka is the unique and high sign of victory of virtue over vice, truth over false, human over demon. So Hindu people regard Lord Ram Chandra is god of great power and people worship him for power to get victory over evil and devil living beings. The birth day ceremony of Lord Ram is observed as National religious festival in Nepal. This great day is known as Janma Astami, the eight day of lunar calendar in the month of Chaitra. Hindu people on the auspicious day pay homage to Lord Ram. People on this holy occasion worship Lord Ram with hope of happiness and success in life. On the eve of this religious day people would be busy in performing Bhajan Kirlan for salvation. It is the habit of the devotees to pronounce Lord Ram to get free from misery in life from evil spirits and black and harmful spirits. On the oceanic Hindu religion, the Ramayan is the extra ordinary religious Epic liked by Hindus to read to learn many valuable moral and ethical lessons that are more valuable and powerful than gold, silver, diamond etc. to build the character of the people as ideal one. One must read this holy book 'The Ramayan' to know in detail about Lord Ram and his virtuous action for humanity and his victory over demon monarch Ravan. All ups and downs of life of lord Ram plainly describes in this great book.

Lord Brahma :—Lord Brahma is another great of power in the Hindu religion. He is supposed the god of creation. It is mentioned in Hindu religion that all people and all animate living creatures of the world is the creation of Lord Brahma. So all human power is the power of this great god. He is the god of power who filled the earth with various creatures with various power to take this void Earth to Earth of abundance of power. Lord Brahma has created all kinds of creatures good and bad, useful and harmful, simple and complicated and active and passive ones. Creatures of the land of water and of air are the gift of Lord Brahma. Hindu religion says that god Brahma is the supreme of supremes in creation of life in the universe. The only duty of this Lord is to bring life in various shapes and sizes with different manners and nature. Some creatures of Lord Brahma is simple, gentle, sober, beautiful, charming, useful, active, sociable, amicable etc. but some are very harmful, ugly, passive, wild, individualistic, aggressive, complicated, dangerous etc. god Brahma created so many kinds of creatures with so many variations to fill this Earth with multi motion and immotion in the dynamism of this Earth. So, because of so limitless super power of Lord Brahma Hindu religion has placed this god as one of gods of high power.

Lord Ganesh :—Lord Ganesh is one of the great gods of power in Hindu religion. So people worship and pray Lord Ganesh for good days, for happiness and success in life. God Ganesh is the god of benevolence. It is people's belief of heavy rain of property, popularity, gain, success, love and kindness etc. in the life without even a trace of any bad days to shed tears. God Ganesh helps the devotee to put them away from evil eyes. No evil sprits can pour any kinds of problems and troubles in the life of the people whom are favoured by god Ganesh. So people worship god Ganesh to please him to begin any work for getting blessing from this god and with a view not to come across with any misfortune and obstacle on the way to success and gain. Devotees believe that god Ganesh put all obstacles away in people's way to happiness if there appear any obstacles and problems because of evil spirits and harmful black spirits. Being pleased god Ganesh blooms lot of buds and flowers or fruits for devotees to pluck them to lead happy life all the time. So it has been a religious custom of Hindus to put or place an idol of Lord Ganesh in all beginnings of works, in all ceremonies, in all birth days to celebrate or to run the actions. But the formation of body, appearance and movement of lord Ganesh is quite different form other Lords. The appearance is of an elephant body is short and fat. If has an enormous billy. This god can't move in speed. It is said that its favourite pet is mole.

In this centuries old Hindu religion there are many gods and goddesses of power of various capacities quite matchless in the sphere of religion. Lord Indra, Lord Vishnu, Lord Bhairab, god Hanuman god Bhimsen etc. are all Lords of power. They are all gods of unique supreme power of Hindu religion are equally worshipped and people celebrate special great days as religious festivals in their name. Hindu people as their pious duty, would be always busy in, religious performance to pay due homage to those Lords of supreme power to please them so that those gods or Lords would be happy with the people and would rain all good things for bright days of happiness in the Earthy life. There are many goddesses of power that stand in favour of human beings and always function to put evil, devil and all kinds of back spirits that work actively in destroying human beings Hindus pray goddesses of power addressing them 'Mata'. These Almighty goddesses of power are all real divine source of human happiness, success, peace, prosperity, As these are goddesses omnipotent super beings. They in a sincere praying addressing their name, reach everywhere in human beings settlement and flow their insurmountable power to free the people from all kinds of bad and miserable days.

Among innumerable goddesses of different power and capacity of the Hindu religions goddess Durga Bawani, goddess Parbati, goddess Laxmi, goddess Sarashowti, goddess Sita, goddess Radha goddess Kumari goddess of fire, goddess of wind goddess of water etc. are all super goddesses of high divine power. They all have played indescribable power to use for the betterment of human beings and to use it to see the destructive power of evil spirits and all kinds of harmful black spirits. These all Almighty goddesses are symbol of truth, beauty and sanity. People worship and pray these goddesses for their everlasting or life long perennial happiness in life.

Goddess Durga Bhawani :— Goddess Durga Bhawani is the most powerful goddess of Hindu religion. She moves everywhere in human residence when devotees pray her for her wonderful power to use for help and put away all kinds of evil and devil spirits. It is clearly mentioned in the religion how goddess put an end to the demon king Rawan who had been unavoidable hindrance all the time on the way to human advancement. Because of use of goddess Durga's unsurmontable power in the battle between demons and human beings human beings got victory over demon. Goddess Durga Bhawani is such goddess who appears disguising in various divine shapes and sizes with immense power. So this supreme goddess is highly worshipped and honoured for her human welfare steps. All human aspect are touched with supreme power of goddess Durga Bhawani. So everybody every moment everywhere people feel safe and happy under the divine guard of this goddess. The special red letter day for worshipping goddess of power is popularly known as Durga puja festival or Vijaya Dashmi festival. This day is known as Bada Dsahim. This is the national festival of Nepal is celebrated for ten days. All these days people worship goddess Durga Bhawani to possess strength enough for the people to fight with devils, to protect humanity and to remove injustice and tyrannical domination. Hindu people think that goddess Durga Bhawani is the goddess of human freedom and wisdom who is always aware of leading devotees to justice and truth.

Goddess Parvati :—Goddess Parvati is great goddess of power. In Hindu religion this goddess is regarded highly by the people and worship her as great symbol of tantric power. Goddess Parvati saves people from the attack of evil spirits and devil spirits. When people suffer from evil spirits and other all kinds of black spirits people pray with this goddess to save them from such problem. Goddess Parvati hearing the prayer of the people visit in human dwelling disguising in various forms sometimes as ordinary human being and use her super power to finish off the evil and black sprits. According to Hindu religion this goddess of Himalaya has impartial dealing to her devotees. One who does good service will be gifted or rewarded and punishment for those who do wrong thing to give trouble to other people. So flow of joy and happiness will be provided for good persons and pain and trouble for evil and bad persons. This goddess of Himalya watches carefully all going on happenings in the human world and manage every thing for happy life of the people. If any dilemma occur in people's residence specially in the regions of Hindus this goddess snatches such ugly trouble creating factor to establish hushed and peaceful atmosphere around the living area. In Nepal devotees of Hindu religion pay special homage to goddess

Parvati and they on the eve of Maha Shivaratri worship her equally as they do to Maha Deva for she is a goddess of high power of tantrism and she is the spouse of Lord Shiva.

Goddess Sarashowti :—In Hindu religion goddess Sarashowti is regarded another goddess of power. She is the goddess of learning. So people worship and pay due honour to this goddess to remove their ignorance and innocence. She has power of providing wisdom to her devotees. People worship goddess Sarashowti for wisdom, knowledge and ability which are quite essential things in human life to lead worthy life on the Earth. Learning is way to advance to reality and truth. Goddess of learning provides people the real thing to enlighten themselves and to enlighten the whole humanity. She bestows the power to people to remove human weakness, balance view envies etc. So in Hindu religion goddess Sarashowti is a divine power to provide strength and inspiration of reality in the life of the people. In Nepal a special religion day is marked to perform a ritual Puja (worshipping) to goddess Sarashowti known as (Shree Panchami). On this holy day it is thought that this goddess blesses person to encourage to learn wisdom and knowledge. So people in big crowd visit to the temple of this goddess and pray for good hope and good mind for learning every thing.

Goddess Laxmi:—Another goddess of power in the Hindu religion is goddess Laxmi. It is said that this goddess has unmatchable power to provide the people abundance possession of wealth. In this materialistic world wealth is the best decorative ornament of the people. Those people are considered as people of high fortune when they are favoured by goddess Laxmi. People worship goddess Laxmi to please her so that she enters in their house and makes them rich. In the presence of this goddess of wealth in the houses of people scarcity turns its tail as wealth dances in magical and musical way. So people offer the favourite things to goddess Laxmi and pray her to bless them to be happy persons in the universe. There is a special great day to be celebrated as great festival to worship and pray goddess Laxmi known as Laxmi Pooja. On this special religious ceremonial day people would be busy in cleaning and decorating their houses to greet this goddess of fortune. Every nook and corner of the house is washed windows and door are decorated with bunches and garland of flowers. At night all houses from bottom to top are illuminated with lights or oil lamps as a sign of joy to greet goddess Laxmi. This goddess of power protects people from trouble and misery by flowing abundant wealth in human doors. This is all short narration of goddess Laxmi.

Goddess Sita :— Goddess Sita is another duly worshipped goddess. She is considered as a symbol of purity. Goddess Sita has power of holiness. She is the spouse of Lord Ram. It is mentioned in the Hindu religion that goddess Sita was kidnapped by demon King Ravan. She was imprisoned for long time in Lanka. In such critical moment goddess had maintained purity and chastity at the cost of life. It is power of purity and chastity of goddess Sita which turned the war between human and demon between virtue and vice for justice to human and to divinity and victory went to lord Ram chandra Bhagawan,. In the kingdom of Nepal. Hindus regard Janakpur zone as a holy place. This zone is a great pilgrim of Hindus for there as a great temple the Ram Janaki temple. Every year on the auspicious day of Ramchandra and Sita's marriage there celebrates religions festival in the name of Ram Janaki Bibha Panchami. The main gods and goddesses of Hinduism as described above are narrated in brief. If people venture to count the number of gods and goddesses in Hindu religion it is sure they will be tired of counting because this number is hard and difficult to count because of many numbers. Foreigners have supposed and called Nepal abode of gods and goddesses. Here numbers of such supreme Lords or gods are nearly fourteen times more than the total population of the country.

In the centuries old Hindu religion there are many mysteries, wonders and amazing super things are hidden which are very hard to know clearly if known they are quite tasty and good to enrich knowledge. People not knowing the limit of the supreme gods and goddess feel surprise in most of the divine activities and in every step they pronounce name of the gods and goddesses for their easy and happy life. Some of their pronunciations are *(a)* Hee Ishwor ! *(b)* Hee Bhagawan ! *(c)* Hee Shambhu *(d)* Hee Mata ! *(e)* Hee Mukti Data ! etc. As Hindu people are sincere to lords on the one hand and afraid of them on the other they spend lot of time in worshipping and praying for gaining power to pass holy life on this Earth. In fact Hindu religion is vast and deep. It is as vast as the sky and is more deeper than the ocean. So the people time to time amaze when they come across with mysterious and unexpected divine acts of the gods and goddesses. Some mysteries in religion of Nepal are firstly people here find Mahadeva in the snow covered peak of the Himalaya known as kailash. They find Mahadiva on deep surface of Goshain Kunda Lake. They find Maha Deva hidden in the ground of their home yard. They call this Mahadeva as Look Mahadeva in short Look Mahadyo. Another surprising fact about gods and goddess of this religion is about demi lord known as Ardha Nareshwor. This lord is peculiar one. Its half body is male in from and half body is female. So it is known as Ardha Nareshwor. This lord has possessed both masculine and Feminine super qualities. Here in this country lord Ganesh also is found in different shapes in various places. Some Ganesh have four hands and some have sixteen hands. In some place there is only one Lord Ganesh in the temple. But in some place there are two lords Ganeshes are known as Joor Ganesh. Here are many such astonishing religious event. If any body take religious Journey in deferent parts of Nepal they have to wonder in their move to different religious centres.

As glimpse of Hindu religion I have presented some great gods and goddess of power and their wonderful and unmatchable tantric power used time to lime in this universe as unexpected miracle. This religion has embraced many gods and goddesses that are very difficult to write and to remember their name. But whatever the size of the religion it may be people must accept it that Hindu religion is quite weighty and worthy to appreciate its value.

The tongue of Hindus of Nepal moves to pronounce 'Tiatish koti Devata' means thirty three hundred millions gods and goddesses. Among so many Gods and goddesses some other major gods and goddesses of Nepal are (1) Bhairab (2) Lord kumar (3) Narayan (4) Bhagabaties (5) kalees (6) Vijeshswori (7) Gujeshwori (8) Yama god of death (9) Bajra yogini (10) Bajra Barahi (11) Bandevi (goddess of forest) (12) Mahnkal (13) Karkot Nag (14) Manokamna Mai (15) Machendra Naths. One is white face and another is red face (16) Surya Narayan (sun god) (17) Chandrama (moon goddess) (18) Dharati Mata (The Earth goddess) (19) Kumari (The living goddess)

As it is not possible to write the name of all supreme gods and goddesses many other names are left. All names çan be compiled only after hard labour. Even counting all names of gods and goddesses is as difficult as counting stars in the sky. My purpose of this writing is not only to narrate all gods and goddesses and their tantric capacity but to present a new approach of mine in the field of tantrism which is totally antagonistic in all respects. But before being busy in my own topic I want to narrate briefly about Buddhism. Buddhism is propounded by Lord Buddha 2546 years ago. This religion is quite scientific in comparison with Hindu religion. So it is more practical and effective and more comprehensive than the philosophy of Hinduism. Prince Siddhartha Gautam, son of king Suddhodhan and queen Maya devi of shakya clan had propounded this Buddhism. How Siddhartha, Gautam founded Buddhism is a matter of dedication on the one hand and fruit of long hard effort and uncommon sacrifice of prince Siddhartha Gautam on the basic of human suffering on the other. Buddha is a man first and Lord second. He is promoted from man to Lord. I have ventured to write a few pages about high and extra ordinary religious works of Lord Buddha to make clear what contribution praiseworthy to all people is done by Siddharth Gautam in religion. By denouncing every human link, princely joy and happiness, well and woe of life and all comforts and luxuries Siddhartha Gautam left the palace of king Suddhodhan with a view to find out truth of the universe. He moved here, there and every where in search of peace and truth. He practised meditation for long time to put his mind in his own control. In search of reality of life, occurrence of different kinds of miseries and diseases in human life and panacea like peace to find out for joy of life he, willingly, was ready to get physical pain and hardship. For unknown success he abandoned all things of life to breathe as simple human being. Help of material things went away from him. On the way to success of enlightening the world Siddhartha Gautam faced many hard obstacles, which can't be tackled by ordinary persons of tolerance. He passed time in fasting for many days, gave hard troubles in his body to concentrate his mind and soul. After a long abstract chain of events, all of sudden, on the full Moon day (Poornima) he succeeded to enlighten himself and to enlighten the world. Form the vary Full Moon day an ordinary prince became Lord Gautam Buddha. He became the Lord of peace in the world. By birth though Siddhartha Gautam is a man born in silver spoon family because of his supreme extra ordinary duty in many walks of his life succeeded to be a Lord-Lord of peace and truth. Within the frame of centuries old rigid Hinduism Buddhism appeared as a beautiful and bright everlasting star in humanity. Sweet scent of Buddhism, spread to many countries of Asian continent first and slowly it covered other continents of the world. Lord Buddha is light of Asia. The upward and forward motion of Buddhism touched every where of the globe and reached to the United Nations Organisation. The United Nations has recognised Buddhism an essential religion to maintain peace and unity in all parts of the world. It is the five principles of Buddhism that tackle any complication in human society because of war and fighting between or among the countries of the world. I do not want to swim in the vast ocean of this religion. My only intention of presentation of Buddhism in this writing is to display its wonderful super quality of spiritual flying that is concrete tantric power of this religion. The high tantric power of this religion is its tantric quality. The great Buddhist monks and sincere devotees of this religion through meditation being under strict codes of this religion fly spiritually to far distance. They used to fly from one country of another, from one region to another. Because of such high spiritual flight Buddhist monks, devotees of Buddhist countries as Srilanka, Thailand, Burma, Japan etc. have reached in Nepal. This is certainly the tantric power of Buddhism. Again healing of different unknown and undiagnosed diseases by moving hands in magical way, by sprinkling holy spelled water over the body of patients and by offering holy spelled water to drink, by marking on forehead of the patients with spelled ash, by hanging jantra round the neck of the patients etc. are all tantric methods of Buddhism. All these tantirc beauties can be shown by Buddhists monks, sages and devotees. In Nepal here are many Buddhist tantrists who were highly capable for their activities. Such tantrists are found in all clans of Buddhism or Buddhist family. Among many Buddhist tantrics many years ago there was a great tantric figure in Bajrachry clan. He is none but 'Jamana Gubhaju' (A person who never ate rice in the life) from the very birth to death this Jaman Gubhaju never ate rice was a wonderful great Buddhist tantric of Nepal who had shown many high tantric miracles in the country. He was Jamana Gubhaju who could change himself into a bird or an animal. He had healed many persons and had established many tantric shrines in the country. Here were many Bajracharya tantrics, Gurung tantrics, Lama tantrics, Bhote tantrics of Buddhism who had done many healing works to hold holy social services. Some tantrics used to hold social services. Some tantric used to fly in the sky being a pigeon, some walked beings a tiger and some visited other person's house being a cat. Certainly such phenomenons are tantric phenomenons of Nepal. Even at present such expert tantrics persons are found in Nepal.

All know it that Nepal is the birth country of Lord Buddha. 2546 years ago Lord Buddha was born as a prince named Siddhartha Gautam in Lumbini zone Kapilbastu district of Nepal. Nepal is proud of getting such great Lord of peace as son of the country. People of Buddhists countries as Japan, Thailand, Srilanka, Burma, China are eager to visit in Nepal to see the holy birth place of Lord Buddha. Governments of such Buddhist countries have helped Nepal to develop Lumbini, the birth place of Lord Buddha as a small heaven on the Earth. So they are always ready to donate all kinds of things, money, human resources. No doubt, Lumbini is an everlasting national pride of Nepal is recognised by the world.

In fact, Buddhism is not the religion of fear and tear rather it is the religion of devotion and meditation. This religion proves that labour is seed to grow sweet fruit. This is a sweet religion which is full of sweet juice as energy power of action and reaction. No one is forced to adept this religion. This is a scientific religion. If one finds benefit one can adept it if one can't find any good thing in it can leave it. The motto of Buddhism is no killing, no cheating, no troubling, no violence no hate etc.

I am putting down some more about Buddhism to gain faith from people of the world. As this religion is scientific, simple, no mystery, no patches of clouds of doubt, easy to follow, Lot of tantric calibre etc., People of Buddhism in Japan, Srilanka, Thai Land, Burma, China etc. have got more things of sanity in the life. They have found more miracle spiritual purification, spiritual flight, mental peace and mysterious tantric power. People believe Buddhism, is a simple way to salvation. Unlike others religion Buddhism is the simplest and scientific religion. As in science it is quite applicable in action. This is a practical religion. Anybody can taste it practically. Nobody is compelled to take this religion. Every body can take it if they like it. There is only one god in this religion that is Lord Buddha. But people find various positions of Lord Buddha and various religious codes and religious performances to enjoy various religious vitality, morality, unity, tolerance, peaceful existence etc. In other religions there are many gods and goddesses. So followers, devotees and sages or hermits have to worship them all equally and have to pray differently for different things. They have to be in fear that god and goddesses would be angry with them if they could not follow all religious codes properly. Time to time devotees, followers and sages get boon and curse from those supreme lords and have to fall sometimes in joy and sometimes in sorrow. But the devotees, followers and monks of Buddhism are free from such religious impact because of Lord Budha's scientific approach, simple and humanitarian sermons and service oriented virtue. As this religion is quite in keeping with human nature and way of human life many people of the world liked it and adopted it as good religion. Buddhism is effective religion theoretically and practically for it has no unnatural, undesirable and unbelievable wings. Many Buddhist monks who are known as Viskchhus have various kinds of tantric power that are used in time of need to heal diseases. When people suffer from incurable diseases medically many of them are cured by the use of tantric power of Buddhist monks. This is the real value of Buddhism. There are three different doctrines in Buddhism they are all Yanas which is known as Triyana. They are *(a)* Hinayana *(b)* Mahayana and *(c)* Vajra yana. These are the best means of attending enlightened in Buddhism. All followers of this religion must follow these yanas for peace in their mind and peace every where in the humanity. People liked and followed panacea like doctrines of Buddhism, for peace and salvation. Again this religion is rich in tantric miracle that's why Buddhist monks and Viskchhus since the very early time had practised tantric ritual spells using useful doctrines. Now I have presented two pictures. One is the abode or temple of Lord Buddha and another is meditation pose of Lord Buddha. It is my hope that these two pictures create miraculous unquenchable thirst to learn more about Buddhism to add virtue

Lord Buddha

Birth of Lord Buddha

in the life of the people. And people will venture to swim in the ocean of peace and non-violence for lasting happiness bloomed in sanity and truth to put away all weakness selfishness, ignorance, ugly, giving up killing of other creatures and harmful Ego. From the very boyhood prince Siddhartha Gautam was highly influenced from the going on various events, he had seen in different time people being old, diseased and death of human life. These on going horrible and unpleasant, sights evoked prince Siddhartha Gautam to be wonderful and dashed him to move far and wide in search of truth and peace by giving up all princely comforts. His uncommon will to find out the true reason of being human beings old, diseased, death and ascetic could not be avoided by any material things and leaded him to the high way to be Lord. The chosen way by prince Siddhartha Gautam for success and salvation was very difficult and hard. But their prince was never despair. Journey to this infinite realm was continued until sweet success was found. In reality, Buddhism is the outcome of Lord Buddha's hard labour. So this religion is practice oriented religion and has tantric flavour. The founder of this religion, in fact, has not intended to pour fear, tear, doubt and suppression of human beings in it. He has poured pure toil in search of peace and truth to make people rid of their fantastic, uncertain and unnatural dealing and feeling. This is the real beauty of Buddhism.

The world has recognised Nepal as Lord Buddha's birth place and the Buddhists country. Hinduism and Buddhism are tow religions of equal length, breath and height of the people of Nepal. Both religions go hand in hand for the upliftment of the people. This is a unique glory of Nepal and people of Nepal are proud of such religious harmony. Buddhists want to see Buddhism bloomed sweetly in Hinduism in all countries of the world. But because of wrong interpretation, misunderstanding domination of individual immaturity, selfishness and greediness of the followers and devotees of Buddhism this religion could not flow every where smoothly and strictly on the path. It is a great matter of regret for the people of Nepal specially for sincere and devoted Buddhists. But both Hindus and Buddhists of Nepal have wished and hoped that both going on religions would flourish on soil of humanity for ever and the tantric practice will be used effectively to heal all complicated unseen and undiagnosed diseases and anxieties lingering since centuries successfully in high psychological way to add value of this kind of practice.

It will be better to present some important means to perform ritual acts of Hinduism and Buddhism in simple picture. Those very essential means are *(a)* Bell *(b)* Damaru *(c)* Sankha *(d)* Bead *(e)* Bajra *(f)* Sukunda *(g)* Thanka *(h)* Dholak *(i)* Tinchhu *(j)* Dheimai *(k)* Kaa *(l)* Trisul *(m)* Muralee *(n)* Jhyali *(o)* Mukha *(p)* Madala *(q)* Khadga *(r)* Damaha *(s)* Jolanhaken *(t)* Kota *(u)* Gulpa

MEANS TO PERFORM RITUAL ACTS.

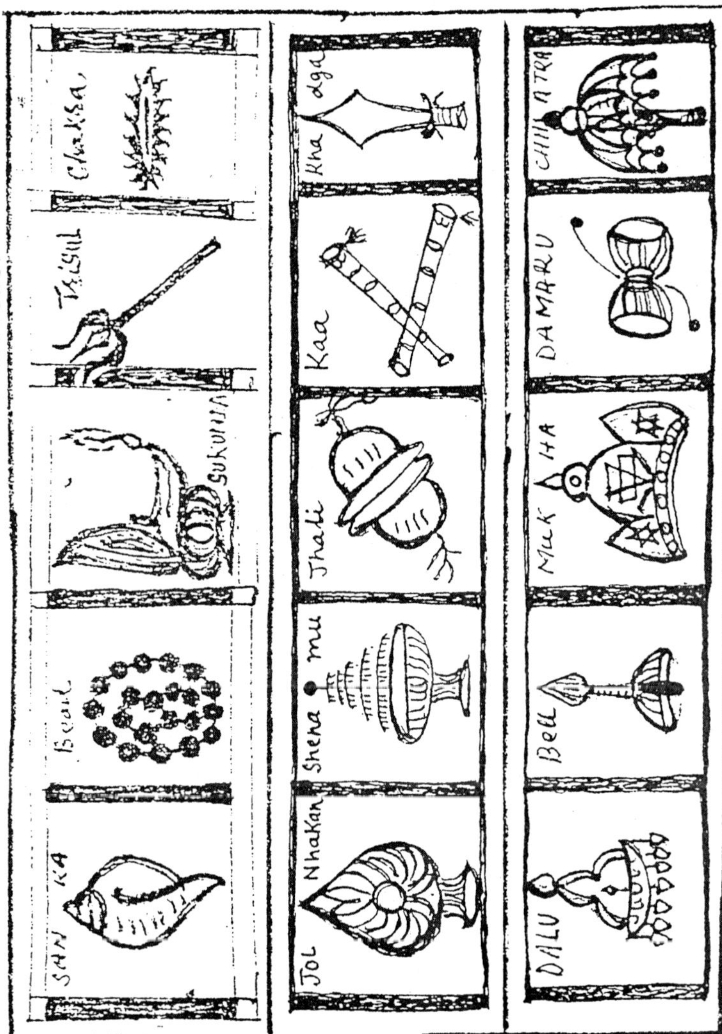

(v) Chhatra *(w)* Kalas *(x)* Patra *(y)* Ritual dress *(z)* Palla, Lapesh, Saleen, Tahpeen, Pujava that (Plate for suting all things to worrship) etc.

Gate keepers of the Temple

All religious mean and instrument mentioned above are very essential things to perform religious ritual performance. In Hinduism and Buddhism those all means are used equally and properly for effective ritual work. But only difference in these two religions is in Hinduism animals such as goat, buffaloes, cocks, draks, are killed to offer gods and goddesses by Hindus to please them with hope of getting blessing from supreme lords. But in Buddhism Buddhists never kill any kinds of animals to Lord Buddha. According to Buddhism such offering of animals is strictly prohibited. Lord Buddha's principle is 'Live and Let other live'. So in his preaching Killing animals for religious performance is not allowed. Lord Buddha is great preacher for relief from pain, misery, mental anxieties. Now Lord is regarded as Light of Asia, messenger of peace, harbinger of non violence.

There are some remarkable things worthy to mention are care takers and gate keepers of the temples or abodes of gods and goddesses. Every temple whether it belongs to Hinduism or Buddhism has been taken great care by the care taker who is known as Pujari. Pujari's duty is to put the temple neat and clean and manage religious activities to the people. Again the caretaker will take care of all properties of the gods goddesses. Another thing is the gate keeper or guard of the temple. Just out side the main gate of the abode of gods and goddesses there are kept a couple or pair of gate keepers. Those keepers are kept both right and left side of the main gate of the temple. Those gate keepers are in some temple *(a)* Lion *(b)* Elephant *(c)* Horse *(d)* Bull *(e)* Angel *(f)* Dragon *(g)* Peacock *(h)* Disciple of gods and goddesses *(i)* Mole. Those gate keepers are made of stone or metal or of wood. Since ancient time in both Hinduism and Buddhism in the main gate keepers have been kept. Lions on both sides of gate Angles and dragons also are found at the upper side of the gate. They are put in a attractive style that are appreciated by visitors as unique beauty of the temple in some temple even great followers, disciples and devotees are also found as gate keepers of the main gate of the holy spot, the temple. In Buddhist temple visitors find Buddhist monks (vickhus) in the religious uniform standing on both sides of the gate. In the Buddhist monasteries people can see great Lama monks (vickhus) standing as gate keepers. In other words they are known as Dwar pal. In some temples snakes are used to decorate gate. In the temple of Lord Ganesh moles can be seen as gate keepers. The elephants and the horses are kept as the keepers of the temples. Again in some abode of gods of great power bull is kept as the keepers of the temples. Again in some abode of gods of great power bull is kept as Guard of the temple and in some temples it is kept as a loyal watcher to see the going on events within the boundary of Lord dwelling. In the temple of Lord Mahadeva of Pashupati temple there is kept a big bull just in front of the main gate facing to Lord Mahadeva. This is all a brief narration about the gate keeper and watcher of the temple.

Now I write a few lines about kumari, the living goddess of Nepal. In the history of religion it is narrated that goddess kumari is the daughter of Lord Bhairab. This living goddess lives in her adobe known as kumari Ghar by durbar square at Basantapur of Kathmandu. She is regarded as living goddess of power. People of this country are of the opinion that this living goddess has tantric power. She can visit every where disguising in different shapes. Sometimes she appears as a simple girl in red. Sometimes as helpless poor woman and sometimes as a terrorist to finish off evil and black spitits and as a reliever to the sufferers. This goddess belongs to Shakya clan of Buddhism. This goddess does not leave her home except in a very few special religious occasion. On the great auspicious eve of Indra Jatra goddess kumari is taken around kathmandu valley in a special chariot. This holy day is one of the great religious occasions of Nepal. On this day king of Nepal visits to Kumari Ghar to get Tika and blessing from this goddess. This is another short description of Living goddess Kumari of Nepal.

Now I put down my own view about Hinduism and Buddhism before starting my new approach of tantrism, a concrete step to healing for those who are suffering form evil spirits and black spirits. Hindusim I found is a big ocean of religion in which people could not hold voyage completely. So devotees and followers of this religion fall in confusion, Loss way to salvation, collect fear in the mind and tears in the eyes no concrete return, domination by superstition etc. People are driven sometimes directly and sometimes indirectly by hermits, sages and priests like cattle are driven. No asking or questioning against religious laws and codes though people have pile of doubt and fear in the mind, though they want to measure and taste religious Truth. People have no right to reduce any void sermons and to introduce any new constructive concepts to regulate as additional good sermons. This is the reality of Hinduism.

As to Buddhism my few words to pour my opinion are Buddhism is a simple and effective religion. This religion encourages people to be truthful, faithful, helpful, dutiful and useful to all fellow beings and never be fearful, hateful, doubtful and harmful to other. This is the sweet scent and beauty of Buddhism in practice. But because of immaturity of devotees, followers, disciples, and monks and because of their misinterpretation and misunderstanding there grew thick weeds that misshaped this good religion. As time passed on Buddhism, became just like a coconut in the hands of monkeys. It's beauty became just like icebar melted in the hot sun's ray or light. The tantric vigour is lingering dimly and shining without luminous quality. In many Buddhist countries monks of high religious calibre have still possessed tantric strength. They by using this strength, have done useful humanitarian service for human beings who are suffering. Buddhist monks have treated diseases. Some major incurable diseases also have been healed by Buddhist monks with the help of tantirc methods. So in my opinion Buddhist is simple but broad and scientific religion liked by many people of many countries. In fact, religion whichever it may be is brought in practice for the betterment and benefit of human beings. Every religion is founded by great persons of extra unmatchable calibre and are ranked as gods by people. After all, religion is brought in practice for peace and happiness of all human beings. Tantric power of the religion is the most effective aspect of every religion. If wicked persons learn the tantric power they use it for misery and trouble of the people. But, if it is learned by good people it will be very useful operation to take people to heal them from unseen, unknown and unidentified diseases. When people suffer from physical and mental weakness or various soft and hard known and unknown diseases that can't be cured by wonderful power of tantrism based on different religions. Healing by means of modern popular medicines is applied in major urban areas. But the tantric healing is popular in rural areas of Nepal. The healing percentage of these two methods in urban areas and in rural areas is shown in the following table

Urban areas	use of medicine	use of tantrism
	70%	30%
Rural areas	15%	85%

In rural areas majority of people believe that people suffer from diseases when they are attacked by evil spirits and black spirits, so people instead of going to physician enter in sage's or monk's house with full confidence that they can solve any problem and can make them free from all sorts of miseries and trouble, Belief or faith is greater than medicine and tantric techniques. But nobody is sure which one is superior-medicine or tantric technique. Both methods have their peculiar power to govern over diseased persons. Those who have belief in physicians go to them to get rid of suffering. Again those who have belief in tantric curing go to sages, monks or hermits and in due course of treatment they would be free from suffering. There is no hard and fast rules to pull and push in these two healing systems. In Nepal when there was no treatment by the physicians by using various mild and hard medicines for curing physical or mental diseases people would rush to monks, sages or hermits for their tantric power to heal them from diseases. The great persons of high tantric power did not use any costly things as medicine rather they would give the patients only very simple things as the spelled water to drink, the spelled ash to mark on their forehead and a kind of power generating thing to hang round the neck which is popularly known as Jantra. Mostly Tantric persons treat the patients for some days and make them completely free from suffering. But in old cases more than seven days they take to cure them. This tantric treatment either belongs to Hinduism or Buddhism is very cheap and wonderfully effective. This kind of treatment plants seed of hope in the mind of the patients that they will be healed soon and there will be spring season on the way to their life. But because of passing of time science arrived here, there and everywhere in the world flapping it's wings of reason. The religion though it is older by centuries slowly began to loose its strength of tantrism and slowly it began to fade away. Such passive impact is not only on Hinduism and Buddhism rather it is on other major religions of the world. The introduction of science and technology played vital role in human life. They as time passed on and on brought changes in human outlook, thought, belief etc. As the result, yesterday's sweets became sour to day. To day's sweets become sour. To days truth may be false in coming days. To morrow's hope may die in it's own womb. So on this wonderful and mysterious Earth religion also may and must change its colours, shape, strength etc. for upward and forward swing. So in religious swings people must know when to swing, how to swing and how long to swing to enjoy it much. At present in Nepal people have not used religion properly for religious purpose. It is used only to prove that they are good and virtuous persons. Now in Nepal religion is used as fashion show to march in the line of virtuous persons so that they could collect respect, honour, love and help from other people. The regular motion of religion is moving in all human dwellings as normal performance of the people and has been turning to gloomy path. If effort is not done to turn it to bright side religion will be just like a bony thing that can't be chewed by the coming generation and it may vanish in the soil. In such situation tantrism also will be no where in the world to be used for healing of unknown and mysterious diseases.

Any subject whether it is science or religion is man made thing is made for healthy and satisfactory moral development in the life of the man. Every thing may not be totally good or totally bad rather it is mixture of good and bad thing. So in use of every thing man should filter to thresh out bad thing to enjoy good quality. Religion is good thing for the people to be virtuous, honest and spiritually rich. Science is good to be strong in constructive wit and power to utilize for human development by producing fine, good and laboriously capable men. But what is wished and hoped can't be obtained and fulfilled in the realm of science too. If science is not used carefully and properly it is destructive. It destroys the world and in the long run this Earth will be empty and naked. When science will not be active to bring every good thing combined with culture customs, tradition, morality, Love, sympathy, unity, co-operation peace etc. the religion will move forward to manage every good thing in the world. It is religion that enriches men in love, friendship, truth, honesty peace etc. by flowing virtue. As the result, all people will come back to human train track and every nook and corner of the world will be again full of peace and prosperity. Every religion has more or less tantric power which is useful for better life. It is used for people to make them free from all kinds of problems. People by nature because of following weaknesses as envy, enmity, selfishness, anger etc. intend to pour sufferings in other people by using evil spirits and black spirits. Some bad or wicked people plant and cultivate bad things in their mind, such people never want to see joy of the people, never want to hear laughing of other persons rather enjoy much in weeping, shouting in pain, crying for help etc. It is tantric power of the religion applied very carefully to root out trouble of the good, simple, gentle and honest people caused by bad and wicked people. So the tantric power of the religion is brought in practice and is taught to the people as a good means to check up the poison like activities of wicked persons, evil spirit and black spirits. My tantrism is a research venture to put in light with holy view to mitigate all sorts of bad spirits, evil spirits and all kinds of black spirits. But my this research in this field is quite successful to kiss the sky. I hope the hanging fruits and blooming flower of my effort will be sweet to all healthy and wealthy persons and it will be panacea for all kinds of problems and miseries of the human beings. My research in tantrism, is positive, reformative, simple and clear. It is positive, reformative, simple and clear. It is helpful and hopeful for those who are suffering form evil spirits and black spirits. I have, after enough research in this field, originated some methods or rules to get rid of going on unseen and mysterious problems because of evil spirits and black spirits. My healing method is quite different from old tantric methods. My methods are quite contradictory to every aspect of old popular rules and methods. My all methods and rules that I have presented to those who have great interest to apply are preventive ones not positive at all. Old tantric healing solely base on religion is purely positive. In old methods gods and goddesses of power are worshipped to borrow divine power from Lords. But in mine no need to worship the gods and goddesses of power. In my tantric healing only meditation is essential. It is totally atheistic. But in some cases which are hard and very old to cure the old methods like but not the same are applied. Nepal is known as an abode of gods and goddesses since the time immemorial people have been punished when they did not follow the divine sermons of gods and goddesses to lead normal peaceful life, when they would perform some kinds of inhuman actions to trouble whole community, when people could not satisfy Almighty gods and goddesses by offering things etc. Nepal is a famous country of tantrism. Here are many extra ordinary tantric works full of wonder and surprise performed by great tantrists. Earthquakes were stopped, heavy rain for long time was stopped, famine, epidemic disease spread in the country was checked, scarcity was replaced by abundance, terror is changed into peace, disguised human as cat, dog, tiger and any other animals etc. are good evidences of tantric performances of different time. Among many great tantrists Jamana Gubhaju is the greatest. Jamana means does not eat rice; He, from his birth till the end of his life never tock or ate rice. Only fruits and vegetables are his food to live on. His tantric performances are so high, unique, great, miraculous they are very difficult to describe exactly. To make more clear about high power of the greatest tantric person Jamana Gubhaju among the great tantrists of Nepal have put down some potential tantric works of him though they are not recorded systematically and authentically in the historical postulates. It is said once Jamana Gubhaju to show his tantirc wonder had sent his disciples to take water in a netted bamboo basket. His disciple filled the basket with water without even a drop leakage. It was carried by him. This was the most extraordinary demonstration of the tantric power of his time. It is also said this great tantric person of Nepal according to the need for his action can disguise in any form. He can fly in the sky as an eagle, can walk and enter in any human residence as domestic animals as cat, dog he flew as an eagle to take revenge on a foreign tantrist who had visited in Nepal to show his tantric wonder had indirectly challenged him. The foreign tantrist was afraid of him and ran away from the country immediately. Jamana Gubhaju's tantric power is a miracle. He can easily bend the mature branch of a big tree by pulling it by his toe. Jamana Gubhaju's wife also had great power of tantrism. It is said she used her own leg as wood to burn for the preparation of wine. Nepal has many tantric persons belong to different castes and clans. It is also mentioned in the tantric history of Nepal that Surat Bajra Bajracharya son of Tachhe Bahal was once attacked by a great Lama. Tantrist of Nepal saved his life using his best tantric power. He is still remembered by the people of the country as a pleasure for his remarkable tantric power. The people of high land of Nepal have also many powerful tantrists. In the communities of Gurung, Raj and Lama there are many tantrists who have shown many remarkable tantric power. They are also quite expert in this field to put away any kinds of physical and mental problems with the help of tantric power. Tantric ritual codes or laws are known as Mantras in Nepali Language. Most of the mantras are formed in religious laws and made of seven Letters. Some are made of nine or eleven letters. Many mantras begin with high spell of virtuous letter 'OM' 'ॐ' and end with 'Hum Phat' 'हुं फट्', Tantrists meditate mantras silently but emphatically to use them highly effective. They in every moment of meditation of mantras concentrate their attention to gather physical and mental power to pour solidly over the patients. Most of the tantric persons by meditating secret mantras throw short breaths three to seven time in one attempt over the patients to make them free form the evil spirits and black spirits domination over them mercilessly to create pain and problem. In the healing procedure tantrists whether they are lamas, sages, hermits, Thakalies, Jhakrays, Dhamis or women incarnated as goddess known as Dyoma, Dyomaiju use ash, broom, spelled water, uncooked rice, scented burning stick or insane which is known as dhupa in Nepal Language, raw thread, chilli, charcoal, peacock's tail feather, earthen pot, nut, Mandala, beans of various types, soil and sand, Jantra a special body guard like thing made using secret mantras given to the patient by the tantrist. Domesticate birds and animals such as duck or drake, cock, goat, pigeon, egg, common fruits and flowers etc. are also essentials. By using all these mentioned things above or some of these things according to need for healing all healers whoever they may be treat the patients. Time for treatment is three to seven days. If the patients strictly follow the directed things to them by the tantrists or healers he/she will be free from any pain and misery caused by evil spirits or black spirits. Tantric healing is century old healing. Many people believe in such healing so they gather around the tantric healer with hope and faith that they will be free from any sorts of pain and miseries. But in different tantric healing methods the process more or less seem to be similar but mantras, tantric spell of secret code or law vary in each tantric healer. The specific qualities of code and laws of century old tantric healing are full of orthodox, mysterious, private or personal and unquestionable. Most of those codes are completely gods and goddesses based. To be effective in the application of tantric codes or laws first of all tantric healers had to please gods and goddesses by offering drack, cock, goat etc. and high worshipping to start their action by spelling holy mantras silently and breathing shortly form three to seven times in every attempt. They continue this process in a short gap of few minutes in each healing step. Belief of the patient in the healer stricks rigidly and hope of recovery from the disease grows steady in the mind of the patient. This is the proper doctrine of the old tantrism of Nepal. What I have described in this writing from the beginning to this point is the totality of tantrism of Nepal applied coloufully and zig-zagly in the old religion. When I viewed old traditional tantrism from different angles in deferent time I found some of techniques and procedures of it are of high weight but most of the tantric codes are surrounded by thick black clouds, thick fog and invisible mists. Again there is lack of clear cut understanding and comprehensive follow up, that's why ordinary persons can't learn it easily. Most of the mantras and tantric codes are concealed in the traditional tantrism. Because of not bring in light all documents, codes, popular and easy criterions it is sinking slowly to vanish. If it is preserved, it will be more valuable than diamond to flow perennial harmony in human dwelling. But it has not been so. I hope this old Hindus and Buddhists tantrism move effectively and people get maximum benefit from it.

I have divided tantrism in Nepal in two sections. A and B. Section A is for old tantrism that belongs to Hindusim and Buddhism. Section B belong to my own tantrism. Now I have ventured to present my own tantrism. It is my new approach in this field is solely product of my research. It is totally different from old one. My intention of holding research in this field is to free the people from evil spirits and black spirits. I am sure if people follow all directions that I have given in this book in right moment and right way nobody will suffer form witches, wizards, all kind of abnormal and unnatural spirits and all other kind of evil spirits. So placing full stop in the old traditional tantrism I step forward with my new tantrism to control or remove all evil spirits and black spirits one by one systematically. Hope it will be helpful to all people.

I have presented some pictures of gods and goddesses of power of old Hinduism to make know the people of other religions how these Lords and goddesses have affected in the normal life of the human beings.

Gods and Goddess of power

Lord Maha Deva and Goddess Parvati

Lord Krishna and Goddess Radha

Goddess Durga Bhawani

Living Goddess Kumari

Lord Gautam Buddha

Lord Ram and Goddess Sita

Lord Ganesh

God Laxman

God Hanuman

Swet Bhai Rab

Praying Hanuman

Goddess Laxmi

Palanchok Bhagwati

Three faced Shiva

Chariot of white Machhendra Nath

Standing Lord Ganesh

Goddess Sarashwati

Some collected high, Holy and secret ritual spells of power of religion and tantrism.

I have, holding continuous hard labour in the field of different religions and tantrism for years, collected some high, holy and secret ritual spells of power that time to time affects in human life for well and woe, happiness and misery, laughing and weeping, rise and fall, turning and betrayal, reward and punishment etc. My colleted some high holy and secret ritual spells are as following.

1. Om Akhanda Shakti Hum Fata. (ॐ अखण्ड शक्ति हूं फत्)
2. Om Khanda Khanda Akhanda Shakti Hum Fata. (ॐ खण्ड खण्ड अखण्ड शक्ति हूं फत्)
3. Om Shakti Shati Mahashakti Hum Fata. (ॐ शक्ति शक्ति महाशक्ति हूं फत्)
4. Om Khandoroya Hum Fata. (ॐ खण्डोरोय् हूं फत्)
5. Om Chgaman Pantan hum Fata. (ॐ च्यामाँ पान्ताँ हूं फत्)
6. Om Laman Pantan Hum Fata. (ॐ लामाँ पान्ता हूं फत्)
7. Om Shyaman Pantan Hum Fata. (ॐ श्यामा पान्तां हुं फत्)
8. Om Shwantan Fantan Hum Fata (ॐ श्वातां फान्तां हुं फत्)
9. Om Hang chashang Hum Fata (ॐ हाङ च्यासाङ हुं फत्)
10. Om Akash Deep Hum Fata (ॐ आकाश दीप हुं फत्)
11. Om Patala Deep Hum Fata (ॐ पाताल दीप हुं फत्)
12. Om Ghring Ghring Shring Hum Fata (ॐ ध्रीङ ध्री. श्रीङ हुं फत्)
13. Om Dukha Mochan Shakti Hum Fata (ॐ दुःख भोजन शक्ति हुं फत्)
14. Om Kantan Fantan Hum Fata (ॐ कान्तां फान्तां हुं फत्)
15. Shree Karkut Nagrajara nama (श्री करकुत नागराजाय् नमः)
16. Shree Akhanda Jyoti Nama (श्री अखण्ड ज्योति नमः)
17. Shree Danava Nashenee Nama (श्री दानव नाशीनी नमः)
18. Om Kali Kali Mahakali Hum Fata (ॐ काली काली महाकाली हुं फत्)
19. Om Pap Mochan Shakti Hum Fata (ॐ पाप मोचन शक्ति हुं फत्)

20. Shree Kal Mòchan Shakti Hum Fata (श्री काल मोचन शक्ति हुं फत्)
21. Om Har Har Mahadeva Nama (ॐ हर हर महादेव नमः)
22. Shree Ganesha Namo Nama (श्री गणेशाय् नमौ नमः)
23. Shree Lambodaraya Namo Nama (री लम्बोदराय नमो नमः)
24. Shree Mangal Dayak Gananayaka Ganesh Namo. (श्री मंगल दायक गणनायक गणेश नमो)
25. Shree Durga Bhawani Ashur Nashiniya Namo (श्री दुर्गा भवानी अशुर नाशिनिय् नमः)
26. Shree Durga Bhawani Shaktidayani Namo (श्री दुर्गा भवानी शक्तिदायनी नमः)
27. Shree Agni Devataya Nama (श्री अग्नी देवाताय् नमः)
28. Shree Bayou Devatya Nama (श्री बायु देवताय् नमः)
29. Shree Jal Devataya Nama (श्री जन देवताय् नमः)
30. Jaya Shambhu Jaya Shiva Shakaray Namo (जय शम्भु जय शिव शंकराय् नमो)
31. Jaya Ram Sita Ram Jaya Jaya Ram (जय राम सीताराम जय जय राम)
32. Shree Pawan Putra Hanuman Ki Jai (श्री पवन पुत्र हनुमान की जय)
33. Hare Ram! Hare Ram !! Ram Ram Hare Hare (हरे राम ! हरे राम !! राम राम हरे हरे)
34. Hare Krishan! Prabhu Krishan!! Krishna Krishna Hare Hare (हरे कृष्णा ! प्रभु कृष्णा !! कृष्णा कृष्णा हरे हरे)
35. Shree krishna Govinda Hare Murare Hai Nath Narayana Yana Basu Deva (श्री कृष्णा गोविन्द हरे मुरारी हे नाथ नारायण यन वासु देव)
36. Buddham Saranam Gachhami Darmam Saranam Gachhawi Sangam Saranam Cachhami (बुद्धम शरणम् गच्छामि धर्मम् शरमण् गच्छामि) (संघम् शरणम् गच्छामि)
37. Shree Uma Maheshworaya Nama (श्री उमा महेश्वराय् नमः)
38. Shree Haratee Mataya namo Nama (श्री हारती माताय नमो नमः)
39. Shree Manokamana Mai Kee Jaya (श्री मनोकामना माई की जय)

40. Shree Akash Bhairabya Nama (श्री आकाश भैरवाय् नमः)
41. Shree Maha Sarashowti, Shree Maha Laxmiya Nama (श्री महासरस्वती श्री महालक्ष्मीय नमः)
42. Takee Jam, takee jam takee rajo (तकीजं-तकीजं तकी राजो)
43. Shree Nil Barahee Name (श्री निल बाराहि नमः)
44. Shree Bajra Barahee Nama (श्री बज्र बाराहि नमः)

Above given high, holy and secret ritual spells have different religious and tantric power used by the people for different purposes according to their need. Among those spells some are used for praying, some are used for getting blessing from gods and goddesses some are used for gaining tantric power to pour upon other people for good or for bad gain. Again some spells should be spelt silently but some are whispered and some are expressed unknown to other in meditation. But one thing should be clear about such high, holy and secret ritual spells are spells used for praying and begging blessing are spelt loudly and can be heard by other people. But those spells that guarantee power to impose upon other for good or bad are spelt silently in meditating way. Those ritual spells that begin from 'Om' and end in Hum Fata are spells of power are spelt secretly. But those begin from shree and end in Nama are mostly spelt loudly in hymn style are for praying and getting bless from gods and goddesses.

TANTRISM IN NEPAL

Tantrism is a wonderful abstract power of religion. It is found more or less in all countries of the world. It is deep rooted and has high power in Asian countries. Specially in those countries where Hinduism and Buddhism are in high force as directive principles to lead normal human life. Tantrism has been an ideal walk of life. I assure all the readers and all the persons who are suffering form unknown diseases to medical science, all the people who are eager to know about capacity of tantrism and all those atheists who do not believe in such unnatural activities because of evil spirits and all black spirits my this new application helps them to tackle and solve the hard and mysterious pain and problems of different colour which have been too difficult to break them into pieces to bring back human happiness. The main things that I have presented as backbone of my tantrism are (*a*) seven tantric letters unknown to other (*b*) four different Mandalas (maps) of tantrism that indicate pin point of problem and suitable solution of control and root out it. (*c*) The black thread (*d*) Aerial Poles (*e*) guard pot (*f*) Nails (*g*) Char coal (*h*) Soil (*i*) Sand (*j*) Patals of different flowers (*k*) Feather of different black birds (*l*) Different grains (*m*) central bone of matured fish (*n*) rudrakche (*o*) Tiger's skin (*p*) Black soyabean (*q*) Scissor (*r*) black cloth (*s*) Fat of henocious wild animal (*t*) Pure water (*u*) Ash.

By mixing all these pious ingredients this new tantrism provides people sweet fruit as tonic to be free from unknown and undiagnosed diseases whether they are physical or mental caused by bad black spirits and evil spirits. But the patients suffering from disease must have faith in the treatment. Belief is the first and the foremost important factor to get rid of pain and problem caused by evil spirits. The second important thing that the patients should take as their duty is to follow the tantric codes suggested by the healer. In the misuse or abandonment of any one or some codes or rules that they should strictly follow the application of the tantric healing will not be effective or the strength of it will not be effective or the strength of it will decrease. So those who use this tantrism to wipe out all kinds of mental and physical diseases must be as hard as iron to apply all rules and regulations.

Now I put my *(a)* Factor that are the seven unknown tantric letters which are the starting of my tantrism.

(A) The Seven tantric letters

These seven mysterious and meaningful letters are keys to

my tantrism. As in ten commandments of the Bible if one commandment is left there is no use of application of other nine commandments. Similar is the case of these seven letters. Every Letter has its significance and has played very important and unique role. The happy union of the seven letters is the totality of exploration of my new approach in the field of tantrism. It is completely different from the traditional tantrism highly dominated by Hindusim and Buddhism. But in my this tantrism there is no trace of century old religions. In my this 'ism' here is no any old religious strength or power. Only the seven letters are the main root of whole mechanism. This root is so deep that it is spreading with many subroots that can easily bear heavy branches loaded sweet tantric fruits that provide relief to be free from harmful black spirits and evil spirits.

These seven symbolic tantric letters are uncommon letters and unknown to the people. So the significance of these letters are to be explained to make people know how these letters play key role in the tantrism. In this 'ism' there are no any trace of fear, confusion, mercy, blessing etc. of supreme gods and goddesses of the old religions. People are not advised to believe in all kinds of gods and goddesses of power mentioned in the religious book. The real meaning of these seven symbolic letters is if people follow these unknown mytersious letters very carefully by heart, the result will be virtuous and they will be quite safe from all evil spirits and harmful black spirits. In Nepalese societies and communities according to the general conception people are suffering mainly from witches, wizards, ghost, appearing of unnatural fantoms as khyak, Bhuta, Preta, Kankal, Kitchkani etc. People of rural area of Nepal are suffering more from evil spirits as witches wizards, ghosts and Bhuta than the people of urban areas. In the villages people are afraid of witches. There most of the aged selfish widows have learned this secret witchcraft for their safety, for suppression upon other, for earning respect from other persons. It is said one who goes against the will of the witch suffers from different unknown painful disease after getting lot of pain and problem. People of rural area of Nepal are not free from witchcraft. They have suffer much from this craft and want relief from it for ever. But the people of urban have ventured tactically and courageously to cross the tall and strong wall of this evil craft but they are not sure of success. But with green hope they are using education as proper remedy to get rid of such wonderful but difficult thing in life. It has been a custom of the people of educated circle of urban area, though they have fear in the mind of such spirits say that in this scientific and modern age they should not and do not believe in such bad evil spirits. But in fact, the concept of the educated circle can't flow smoothly as truth to tell more about such evil spirits and harmful black spirits. Since the naked life to the clothed life these kinds of spirits have been dominating the people here, there and everywhere of Nepal and other countries and since the stone Age to this scientific developed modern Age people have been victim to such spirits. Science says that all these are pure product of religious superstition and human weakness. But this concept of science is neither totally right nor it is totally wrong. It is rather partly right and partly wrong. In the vast and abstract realm of religion there is enough practical aspect known as tantrism is applied time to time whether it is for good or bad, whether it is harmful or useful and whether it is painful or graceful. So men of wit must measure the maximum limit of tantrism on the one hand and must weight the value of science in it's maximum limit for human benefit. Both the capacity of tantrism and strength of science must be kept in balance for human welfare. But in the practical life of men there have been many obscure dogmatic obstacles. Men of religion always support their own favour and accept its various impacts on life blindly. They never agree the fact that science is another strong force to march on for better life. So they worship the Moon as goddess of beauty and purity. Again men of science never agree anything whole heartedly that are hanging in the branches of religion except things given to them by science. In fact, both religion and science are equally important things for the people for rapid development of the world. Nepal is a highly religious stamped country. Here majority of people have faith in religion. So in good days as well as in bad days people do not rush here and there rather they much to abode of gods and goddesses or visit to those persons' door who are supposed as divine power gifted persons by the god. People hesitate to call on the physicians to solve their problems. This is all because of socio-religious culture of the people of Nepal. So religious performances and tantric healings have been the life bearing powerful device in the country. At present the weight of such socio religious performance whether it is worshipping to gods and goddesses or invisible tantric performance is decreasing due to incorrect application on the one hand and high influence of science and technology on the other. But the faith of the people is still fresh as lingering in still cold water of the lake. Though Herculian task is done from opposite side to put an end the religious activities and tantric action this kind of attempt can't be successful because the people of Nepal have high belief in it and they in their each and every step pronounce the holy words of Lords or gods and goddesses. So instead of putting away such religious act of the people it is better to search a suitable alternative to replace this old and traditional act by using new one.

My this tantric performance that I have presented in this book unlike, other religious performances is centred in seven letters has many beneficial effect that give good impact that never causes any negative result. I AM SAFE is the exact meaning of these  seven meaningful symbolic letters. Now I intend to explain these seven letters one by one to make know people the significance of these letters for their free and prosperous life without even a trace of any ugly and unseen difficulties in human life.

 This is the first symbolic important letter among the set of seven letters of tantrism. This hook like letter stands at the main entrance of the evil spirits and dark or black spirits to

check all of them whatever they may be to enter in the human residence and to hide silently in the human body and human dwelling to scatter potential energy to strengthen vigour of the people to fight with all kinds of evils. This letter again helps people who are suffering from unknown diseases because of harmful influence of bad spirits to be hopeful, to be courageous, to be confident and to be able to face any pain and problems physically and mentally caused by evil and harmful bad spirits. It is a starting letter that pushes persons to be quite capable to use their reason very critically so that they could know what is right and what is wrong. This first letter helps to be active and enthusiastic to be away by forgetting all their fear and tear. One who wants to follow this tantrism he/she first of all must write this letter at least seven times every day. One who becomes able to write this letter accurately in shape and size , I am sure there will grow a kind of wonderful holy feeling of confident that he/she is going to be free from all sorts of downs of life that he/she is going to rise up to pluck three golden apples. One who wants to follow this tantrism he/she must practice regular meditation for required period of time until he/she is able to draw this symbolic letter before the eyes clearly within a minute or less than a minute. How quick it can be drawn solely depends upon practice.

 This second symbolic letter also has its own tantric significance. The value of this letter is to gain peace in the mind and to reach near to success in life being free from the attack of all kinds of evil spirits. In fact this letter is half part of the first letter. First letter is half part of the second letter. First letter encourages feeling of victory, success, prosperity, hope, joy etc. The second letter helps the people to germinate the improved seed in due course of time in the mind of the people. If a person pay more attention to first letter and does not pay equal care to the second letter it will be fruitless and effort spent will be null and void. The second letter pushes first letter forward and pulls it to second letter to bring fullness and completeness. So the person who has desire to use this tantrism for his/her

betterment must know it clearly that seven letters is a chain to be used very carefully to gain maximum benefit. This second letter is co-ordination to the first one. So the first letter is combined with the second one. The power of these combined letters is so solid that evil and black spirits can't centre in the human body to cause harmful pain. The second letter is complementary letter which plays the role of light and pure breathing of life. As in the first letter the person who wants to follow this tantrism must do regular practice of meditation for certain period of time to draw this second important letter before the eyes in no time. He and she must be able to write this letter at a wink to reach to perfection on this topic. This second letter dashes the person in his/her mind to put away any kind of fear, doubt, dejection etc. and replaces them with peace, certainty, hope etc. This is all the short narration of the second letter among the seven letters. As every letter has its unique quality and wonderful power this second symbolic letter also has great power to add some importance in my pyramid of tantrism.

This is the third symbolic letter among the seven letters. It stands against doubt, fear and superstition. In Nepal, but I do not know how far it is applicable to the people of other countries, most of the people sow seed of mental diseases due to their own doubt and fear. When people in Nepal get some bad influence physically or mentally they used to think that evil spirits or harmful black spirits eyed at them and due to it they suffered from various diseases and they disturbed in their mind or on the body. People think many things fantastically and come to conclusion that their suffering has been caused because of sudden and unexpected touch by evil spirits such as witches, wizards, ghost and other many kinds of unnatural phantoms. In fact, people themselves create fear and doubt in their mind and suffer much from such unnecessary fear and doubt. In the beginning people's fear and doubt is mild and simple but soon they will be bigger and harder in the size of the timber. It becomes heavy to bear. Another thing that is more worst than fear and doubt is superstition. It directly penetrate in the mind of the people and becomes the main root to spread various fantastic effect upon the persons. It is superstition which creates horror in the persons for nothing. Because of horror there are loss of reason, loss of all types of necessary and useful potentiality in the person's mind. As the result, people become victim to their own weaknesses, belief in evil spirits and void thinking of every thing in every moment. This third letter helps the people to remove such human weakness. It helps to make mind of the people very strong and energetic. As influence of this letter falls upon persons automatically they will be free from fear, doubt superstition. The matured reason blooms and it will be guide line in the life. But for such potential quality persons must be well prepared for sincere meditation of this letter and must be quite expert in writing letter correctly and beautifully in no time.

 This fourth symbolic letter also has its own peculiarity. It stands for critical thinking of gods and goddesses. This letter enforces the people not to consider deeply the imaginary image of gods and goddesses. In Nepal there are uncountable imaginary image of gods and goddesses in different names. Their shape and size with different capacity are quite amazing. It is critically guessed after deep study that all those imaginary super beings dignified here, there in every nook and corner of the country is creation of wise hermits and sages in ancient time is creation of their imagination because of tears in the eyes and fear in the mind. Such imaginary gods and goddesses though simple in the beginning became a mysterious escape from reality. People believing in such fanciful super beings blindly followed the worshipping and praying with them for every good thing in life. Thick cloud of doubt brought confusion in the mind of the people. They began to cry meaninglessly as a child's crying in the wilderness. This fourth letter encourages people to be away from all. Kinds of imaginary gods and goddesses to be

against meaningless and valueless idols of gods and goddesses. This useful letter, if the people take it seriously and use it in their practice will be fit to cure century old diseases occurred by blind religion, influenced by deductive motion to misery and anxiety and dominated by fallacy over truth. All seven letters presented in this book are of equal value of different calibre. People who have interest are suggested to follow view and concept poured down in this writing to know clearly significance of these letters of tantric vigour. But meditation must be continued regularly so that they could be able to visualise all these unique letters easily. This fourth symbolic and tantric letter also must be drawn in a moment and must be able to write exactly. Use of this letter helps to move to the path of comfort being free from fear of all kinds of mysterious creators such as witches, ghosts, wicked spirits and other all kinds of unnatural spirits and fantoms.

This is the fifth tantric letter. The significance of this letter is of equal important as other symbolic letters. This letter helps to motivate the people to ripen the reason and power for critical thinking specially about the unexpected fantastic evil, black destructive spirits. This is the letter that pushes persons ahead being ineffective by any imaginary image and idols of super beings. This letter also helps to be nondisturbed by any unreasoned, immatured and over matured religious codes or laws. This letter if used regularly and sincerely without reprimand of any high authorized persons, can early achieve to stand in the circumference of reality. In fact, reality is pungent and difficult to digest. If people bear pungency and consume the reality digestively it will be good for sound health and weighty reason to generate the mind of the people smoothly. This tantric letter is an input for required output. As the result, people will be able to be free from all sorts of drawback and problems early on the way to spiritual sanity and supremacy.

 This is the sixth valuable symbolic letter of my tantrism.

This letter inspires the people to get relief form all types of bad, black and evil spirits. It is a symbol of victory over all those evil elements. It encourages people to move near to success in life being free from all kinds of human wėakness as doubt, fear, lack of confidence, over control by harmful super beings, habit of depending upon other. Security, flow of joy, virtuous feeling, clear vision, good dealing etc. are the gain of this letter. How much a person get benefit from this letter solely, depends upon his/her own effort to hold practice of his/her meditation and correct use of this letter. More the use of this letter more will be the profit in life of the people. Pace of happiness travels speedly and people enjoy varieties of Earthly sweet juice of pure fruits. But persons who can't control their mind and can't maintain their normal nature, will not be successful to gain any good thing in this tantrism. But persons of normal temperament can be successful to gain any good thing in this tantrism. To study the value of these symbolic letters. So persons should possess quality of common human nature to learn many things of high value of this sixth letter of the complete set of seven letters.

 This is the seventh meaningful tantric letter. This letter is helpful to add virtuous achievement in the tantric mechanism by putting away all vices which are being ugly and hard obstacle on the way to prosperity, happiness and success in the life of the people. This last letter in the union of seven letters has great role to play for collecting strength of this new tantrism. Persons who want to be free from all kinds of evil spirits must follow all seven letters very carefully and strictly. This last letter must be paid special attention. From the first to the sixth letter are put in order systematically to be effective by this seventh letter. If seventh letter is excluded other six letters can't be in motion smoothly. Though this seventh letter resembles to A alphabet of English language its power and function is different. It has

mysterious tantric power to heal unknown and undiagnosed diseases. If people take this letter with other six letters they can enjoy heavy gain and will be like panacea for them. So I advise all people to use these seven wonderful tantric letters sincerely to change weeping into laughing, despair into hope and pain, problem into joy.

MANDALA

In my tantrism here are four types of Mandalas. They have different roles. These are Mandalas that protect dwelling places of the people. If any evil spirits and black harmful spirits venture to enter at home or in the houses they will be checked by these power bearing Mandalas. These Mandalas indicate the peopl. the arrival of evil spirits as witches, ghosts, and any other black and bad beings. Persons who want to put Mandala at home they must fulfil certain conditions to put it in effective way. Those conditions are as following.

(a) Mandala should be hung to the left wall of the entrance in the room. *(b)* It should be placed at the height of five to seven feet. If the room has enough height place it at the height of seven feet. *(c)* Every night at 7 o'clock either one or seven incenses (Dhupa) should be burnt *(d)* Every Saturday night at seven o'clock Deyo made of black cloth should be used for this purpose *(e)* In the room where Mandala is hung there should not be any kind of idol of gods and goddesses and should not be any picture of gods and goddesses *(f)* persons who are not the member of the family should not be permitted to touch the Mandala *(g)* offering of animals such as goat sheep, buffalos etc. and birds like cock, drack, and pigeon should not be done. *(h)* Lunatics or men of abnormal nature should not be allowed to enter in the room where Mandala is hung. They can be taken in the room only in a condition that is if someone goes with such persons. *(i)* Black thread connected with the Mandala should not be broken or disconnected *(j)* A cover like curtain should be placed

in the Mandala so that strangers or visitors could not make questions about the use of Mandala in the house. *(k)* Any kinds of traditional ritual performance. Should not be done in the room where Mandala is put. *(l)* Mandala should not be removed or changed from this wall to that wall. It should be hung in one wall for ever. *(m)* Mandala should not be fallen from the wall to the floor of the room. If it falls power should be generated in ritual way to make it function again effectively. *(n)* Every morning at seven o'clock simple worshipping to the Mandala should be done. *(o)* Worshipping should be done by offering a white or red flower and seven drops of holy and fresh water. *(p)* Boys and girls below 7 years old should not touch the Mandala. *(q)* the power of Mandala will not be much effective to those men and women who are more than eighty years old. *(r)* Dog, cat, owl, vole, bat etc. should not be taken in the room where the Mandala is hung. *(s)* Every year the black cloth placed behind the Mandala should be changed. *(t)* Blind, deaf, dumb and other disabled persons by birth should not touch the Mandala. *(u)* Hot water, mineral water, impure water should not be used in the Mandala.

These all twenty one conditions should be carefully maintained to use Mandala in the house. If any one limitation or condition is broken there will be mild or soft effect. There may be negative impact too. If many conditions that means more than one condition are broken the functions of the Mandala will be of no action. These twenty one conditions are equally important and equally applicable in all four kinds of Mandalas.

THE FIRST MANDALA (A)

FOR NORTH FACING HOUSE

This Mandala (A) is for the North facing house. Persons of North facing house if are in problem, in anxieties, in suffering from diseases, haunted by ghost, witches, wizards and any other kinds of evil spirits and are physically tired, mentally exhausted, frail etc. due to unsolvable critical condition they should use this first Mandala to be free from all these kinds of problems and sufferings. As this Mandala provides safety and security to the persons and their house, they must place this Mandala to protect them from all sorts of obstacles and problems. If children without any reason for hours cry being astonished seeing uncommon sight and unknown terrible figure, if they feel fear without any reason, if they are sick all of sudden there may be entering evil spirits in the house. Such type of extra ordinary events can't be found if people hang this Mandala. If there flows discontent among the members of the family and conflict among them even in smooth domestic atmosphere, if there is deterioration of health of the persons, unknown disease that could not be cured with the use popular modern medicines it can be doubted that bad and black evil being must have entered in the house or at home. In such case if the Mandala is hung people can get rid of such wonderful event in the house. This Mandala must be connected with antenna and the earthed lines of black thread. All four kinds of Mandalas must be connected in the same way. But this antenna and earthing line are quite unlike to the electric and electronic lines. How to prepare antenna and earth line to connect with Mandala is given separately in another chapter. One important thing about the hanging of Mandala is the Mandala should be hung according to the facing of the house or home. In North facing house Mandala also should be north faced. The same to other three types of Mandalas. The functional power of Mandala can't be fully operative if twenty one conditions are not followed properly and systematically. If people use this Mandala happiness and joy bloom in the house and murmuring laughter adds sweet music in action. No member of the family in the house feels any sort of discontent, weakness, unhealthy disturbance detachment, depression and dejection etc. in the life.

The North facing house have peculiar quality. There is shortage of warmness due to lack of sufficient sun light. So people of such houses of north facing must be cautious of attack of bad and evil spirits. Such North facing houses are in the lack of light, darkness prevails over them. So such houses are favourable place for the spirits that appear in gloomy atmosphere. Again such North facing houses are cold houses. There because of lack of heat for human being people suffer much. As the result, persons of such houses time to time suffer from cold, influenza swelling, cough, pneumonia, etc. diseases. This meaningful Mandala has multi dimensional power. So it can provide people relief to be free from all types of physical and mental sufferings and help to gain required potentialities to grow life satisfactorily. As human fate is personal thing every person must be aware of brightening his/her fate. My this tantric application is a help for the people to turn them to prosperity and success. Certainly my this practical action is a new application unlike the traditional religious action, is positive productive and quite benevolent in action. This 'ism' has no trace of destruction, no trouble bearing, no revenging colour, no fragmentary sign etc. for human beings except ray of hopes and happiness. So nobody should be in doubt and in fear to apply this new thing in his/her day to day action. My this first Mandala is fit only for the people who are living in north facing houses to get relief of all kinds of problems and pain creating evil spirits on the one hand and to introduce all joyful events in the house on the other. So I advise persons to hang this Mandala in the house and follow all conditions to put it in action positively effective. But persons who are conservative followers of any old religions and do not like to bring even slight change in their religious performance they can't get any benefit from the use of this Mandala. But persons who are liberal and responsive to change can enjoy a lot benefits from it.

THE SECOND MANDALA (B)

FOR SOUTH FACING HOUSE

This second Mandala is made for south facing house to keep the house free all kinds of evil spirits. This is the Mandala which keeps away any sorts of suffering, discontent, conflict because of lack of co-operation and co-ordination among the members of such facing house. Again it is quite helpful to get rid of outer attack of wicked and selfish persons. In most of the South facing houses excessive heat may get in and may put negative impact on the people. But such heat is not natural heat rather it is the heat of old religions. Such feverish heat of old religions can influence upon persons to create pain, difficult to cure easily. By hanging this tantric Mandala in the South facing houses persons can check bad and harmful impact to infuse in the house. Members of such houses should not be in fear of unknown and undiagnosed diseases. The pace of life of persons become easy and normal without any disturbance. Due to abstract and un-measurable value of this Mandala persons get great advantages in every tuning of life. They never fall in repentance, reprimand from other harmful persons. They are never checked and never betrayed by other bad persons. This Mandala adds courage and confident in the persons, mind to move ahead for both sweet and sour taste. This is the best Mandala for south facing houses which helps to drop sweet honey drops for the persons if they do sincere and continuous labour straight forwardly following all conditions for the positive operation. The south facing houses get enough sun light. So persons of such houses get less pain and problems from the evil spirits and black spirits. In day time evil spirits can't haunt the house but very powerful spirits rarely get success to influence even in the light of the sun. But at night in complete darkness harmful spirits can enter in the house to play dirty inhuman game. So persons of south facing houses also suffer from evil spirits and other harmful black spirits. But their suffering is lesser than the suffering of the people of other facing houses. So it is better to put Mandala at home to lead life in a simple and better way being ineffective form all kinds of harmful spirits. It is certain that there will be joy and happiness in ever nook and corner of the house if there is hung the tantric Mandala for the south facing houses. In the use of this Mandala persons who are disabled, physically frail, silly in nature mentally depressed etc. also can feel human changes step by step and reach near to normal stage of life. Discontent and miserable persons become content and happy. Shouting like lunatics, weeping and crying vanish in the persons. Spring enters winter runs away in human life. Application is better than hearing description about any thing. So apply it. If it is good put it if not good throw it. This is up to the user of this Mandala. Man saves man and man destroys man. I have used my brain to serve and save men by introducing this new application of tantric conceptual action. Billions of human brains are actively busy in the construction of the world for human beings' happiness and at the same time millions of brains also unknowingly busy in the destruction of the universe. But I claim that I am standing in favour of construction of this human world. My only aim is to hold service to man because service to man is service to god. It is the best service of the man which can grow enough joy for the people of the world.

THE THIRD MANDALA (C)

FOR EAST FACING HOUSE

This third Mandala stands for the protection of East facing house. Persons who are suffering in the East facing houses from evil or evil like unknown and undiagnosed diseases of various types can get relief by the use of this Mandala. People do not know how and when they suffer from bad harmful evil spirits. But they suffer from such disease because of evil and black spirits. These kinds of diseases are unseen and unknown pain and problems for persons. Victim of such diseases is a great loss of health and wealth of the people. People have to pass life in ugly trouble and misery without knowing what to do and what not to do for easy and happy life. Houses of East facing are easy dwelling place for people in the morning time. This type of atmospheric effect last up to noon. As time passes from noon to afternoon bad and evil spirits venture to flap wings in the houses. They silently enter in the houses and wait for suitable time to enter in the body of the people. Abnormality prevails in the house to rule over members of the houses. Pale rays run in the appearance of the persons. No body of the house could decide what to do and how to solve the pain and problems. The effect of evil spirits and their continuous prevailing power in the house will be a hard nut to chew. So persons of East facing houses if hang this Mandala in the residence following all the required conditions they should not worry about any kinds of difficulties. From the very moment of hanging of the Mandala there flows sweet happiness and joy little by little and cater easiness to row the life ship in the ocean of humanity. But for the affective application of this Mandala in such facing houses all those twenty one conditions should be fulfilled otherwise it may not be in action properly. The black time that is deep darkness is the favourable time for evil spirits to haunt the houses and to attack persons. Persons who are suffering from evil spirits must stand in front of the Mandala twice in a day at exactly seven o'clock in the morning and night. They should bow their head with faith and silent praying for relief. This duty to be done by suffers of the North and south facing houses also by paying due attention to such performance for the same relief. But relief from evil and back spirits has been slightly easier than the houses of North, South and West facing houses. East is the sun rising direction. So the sun light is mild warm which affects human body positively and the patients of evil and black spirits become free from suffering soon. One thing more to be sure is persons of East facing house should hang the Mandala in the morning time. The right time is seven o'clock. If there is no sun light hanging of Mandala should be postponded. Rainy day is not favourable day to put Mandala in action. So it must be sunny day to hang Mandala. How much benefit persons get from the application of Mandala depends upon faith of the persons in it. Persons who have no faith in Mandala but used it by force of other person can't get any benefit and will not be able to be free from evil spirits rather they feel great loss. But those who have belief in it must use it as soon as possible. In hanging this Mandala in East facing house persons get sound health and will be happy being free from all kinds of complications created by evil spirits. Evil spirits escape from the house and new evil spirits could not venture to enter in the house. Love, co-operation, understanding etc. will appear in the house. Houses which were full of fear and tears will be happy dwelling places because bad and harmful beings will be no longer existed there. Business houses get lion share profit in short period with the help of this Mandala. One thing more about handing of Mandalas is Mandalas should not be hung within the reach of the children. Children of below seven years old should not touch it. If children touch it they may be ill they may show abnormal temperament. Again the generation of power of Mandalas against evil spirits will decrease if they are eaten by moth. So old Mandala should be replaced by new one.

THE FOURTH MANDALA (D)

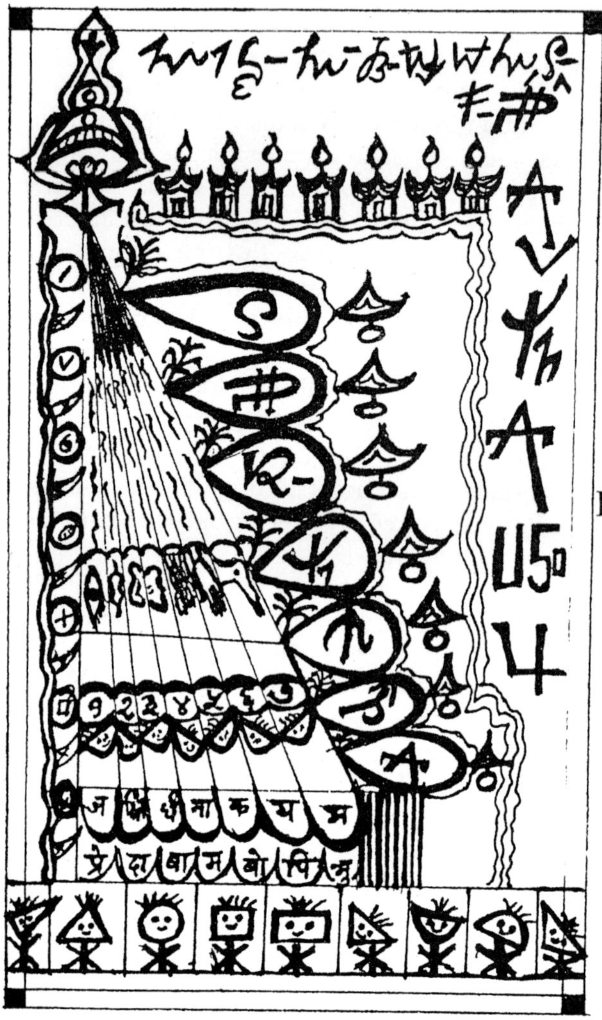

FOR WEST FACING HOUSE

This fourth Mandala is made to use for the West facing house. Persons of such houses time to time suffer from evil spirits and black harmful spirits. Such spirits create many kinds of pain and problems for the people. So persons of West facing houses should hang Mandala to put an end all harmful spirits and all kinds of pain and anxieties created by them in the houses. In such facing houses harmful black and evil spirits often enter and create a lot of various hard problems which evaporate peace in the mind of the people. The harmony among the members of the family also would be destroyed. In the west facing houses evil spirits and all kinds of harmful spirits easily enter with hard wind. When wind blows hardly those evil spirits mix with hard wind and being invisible element they enter in the house and play ugly game to turn luck of the person from good to bad, bright to dark, happiness to troublesome, laughing to weeping in life. Such kinds of miserable condition can't be removed by other persons using popular medicines. The only correct way to be away from such critical and miserable condition is to hang the tantric Mandala at home. This is the Mandala which helps to put away all black and evil power scattered by those evil spirits. In West facing houses persons do not feel any kinds of uneasiness and troubles in the morning. But they feel uneasiness be cause of such spirits only in afternoon time. In such houses trouble and fear creating bad and evil spirits like to enter there. Such harmful evil spirits need hard heat and hard wind to spread their evil power in the house. Both such atmospheric factors are available in enough quantity in West facing houses. Dead soul, the ghost also exist and move strongly in such houses for long time. So persons of such houses time to time feel loss of mental and physical balance. When persons have no mental balance they can't get any joy and happiness in life. They have to face unbearable financial crisis too due to unnecessary expense in removing and controlling evil spirits. As wind blows from west to East sometimes bad smelled smoke of the grave reaches in such houses. So there is more possibility of entangling and entering of dead soul in the houses. If such lifeless souls enter certainly they damage all good and harmonious qualities of human life. So persons of such houses to be happy should use Mandala for being able to save their houses from all sorts of bad and harmful elements. Another thing worthy to mention about such houses is men of wit or man of letters get lot of problems in life to move on. In such condition this Mandala solve this problem created by evil spirits.

TWO MANDALAS FOR DOUBLE FACING HOUSE

Double facing houses need two Mandalas to be hung to get rid of evil spirits and all types of black harmful spirits. Those double facing houses are categorised in the following charts.

A. For East North Facing House
B. For West North Facing House
C. For West South Facing House
D. For East South Facing House

DOUBLE FACING HOUSES

In Nepal here are mainly four types of double facing houses. People of Nepal either live in single facing houses or they live in double facing house. Those who live in single facing house need only one Mandala to hang in the house to get rid of all kinds of evil spirits and black spirits. But those who live in double facing house have to hang two Mandalas for the same purpose. Available two facing houses of Nepal are

A. East North Facing House
B. West North Facing House
C. West South Facing House
D. West South Facing House

The double facing houses are more complicated houses than the single facing houses. In double facing houses double Mandalas should be hung to make the persons free from all kinds of harmful evil and black spirits and to make the house secured dwelling place. In such houses the evil and bad spirits can easily enter to play the dirty harmful games. Evil and black spirits can easily hide and escape when tantric power is imposed over them, so in double facing houses it is very difficult to bring evil and black spirits under control and to put them away from the houses. But in case of single facing houses such complication and difficulties is mild and can be faced. In single facing house evil spirits and all kinds of other harmful evil and black spirits can be removed within few days. But in the double facing houses it takes months to do the same work of relief over the evil and black spirits. Persons of double facing houses are mostly weak mentally through they are strong energetic physically. In decision making on any topic, people of such double facing house fall in confusion and could nor be quick. No quick or prompt moving can be found with them. These symptoms in persons of such double facing houses are because of natural phenomenons on the one hand and haunting of evil spirits on the other. All details of complication and other unique things of double facing houses will be described one to make clear the persons who have great interest in the field of tantrism. It is also advised that people have to change double facing to the single facing house to live to minimise any possible complication caused by the evil spirits.

EAST NORTH FACING HOUSE

Persons of East-North facing houses have to face lot of pain and problems from all kinds of evil spirits. In the morning people feel comfort in life by getting pure sun light. Owing to entering soft and pure sun light or ray from five to twelve in the morning evil spirits and any other bad and black spirits do not enter in the house. From late night to midnight due to lack of sun light in most of the parts of the houses gloominess prevails. Such atmospheric influence is quite favourable for evil and black spirits. Being seen and unseen time to time harmful spirits rule over east-north facing houses and person pass life in fear and tear. Sometimes there enter witches, wizards and another time there appear ghosts, skeleton creatures, fantoms of different kinds, black spirits that pluck mental as well as physical happiness. Peace is replaced by horror, murmuring laugh is vanished and evaporated. Again dwellers of such houses suffer from various diseases that linger sometimes in the head and sometimes in the feet of the persons and become a heavy load for the family to bear on the shoulders. So for proper and correct solution for such mixed problems persons should apply double methods natural treatment by using medicines and tantric treatment by using action oriented religious treatment. Religious treatment is nothing but use of tantric activities to check the entrance of all evil and black harmful spirits. In East-North facing houses two Mandalas should be hung. One is Mandalas for East facing house to be hung Eastern wall of the house and another is Mandala for North facing house. This Mandala should be hung on Northen wall of the house. When these both Mandalas work co-ordinating each other and functions of these Mandalas will be highly effective. As the result, the harmful and evil activities of evil and black spirits will be weak and at last they all will leave the house. Human's all kinds of pain and problems are replaced by peace and prosperity in the house. So advice is given to the persons of double facing houses to use two Mandalas in right time and in right way. People must be eager to hang Mandalas with faith. It is sure that joy of life blooms again to forget unbearable pain and problems easily getting tantric power of the Mandalas.

WEST-NORTH FACING HOUSE

The West-North facing houses unlike East-North facing houses have different easy and hard symptoms. In such houses persons suffer from natural phenomenons and evil and bad spirits. It is hard to solve the problems and pain on persons by evil spirits. Sometimes harmful spirits enter in the West-North facing houses not only through door rather they enter through windows. So evil spirits and harmful black spirits create hard problem for the person of such houses. Mostly in such double facing houses witches, wizards and other harmful pain creating spirits enter in any time. But ghosts and other bad black spirits enter in the house at night. Persons of physically weak suffer much from evil and black spirits. By nature females are mostly attacked by witches/wizards ghosts and black spirits. But it does not mean that male mostly does not suffer from the spirits. But it does not mean that male persons are free from such spirits. Children below five also easily become victim to such spirits. The symptoms of falling witches and other bad spirits upon persons would shout fantastically without reason, weep bitterly for long time closing eyes, unnatural shivering and shaking of body, somnambulism etc. Whether people believe or not to believe in the suffering of persons because of evil spirits and all kinds of black spirits it does not matter. But one who suffers from such incident believe it. One who does not suffer and get pain and problems from events caused by such spirits does not believe it. Person's suffering from disease can be easily cured with the help of physician and give medicine. But in case of unknown suffering caused by evil or black spirits physician and prescribed medicines can do nothing effectively and positively. For the unknown suffering caused by bad, black and evil spirits there is no popular medicine to cure. The best way to get rid of such pain, problems and suffering every one must take the help of tantric treatment. According to tantrism persons of West-North facing houses have to hung two Mandalas. One Mandala is to be hung is the mandala made for west facing houses and another is the Mandala made for the north facing houses. Both Mandalas must be hung properly in right time in right way and in right place being within rules and limitations of the tantrism. Persons of natural vision when suffer from the unknown and mysterious diseases they without any doubt and hesitation must accept tantric application for quick relief from unknown or mysterious disease. So it is my advice to bring favourable atmosphere in the double facing houses of west-north directions as soon as possible by hanging two Mandalas of tantrism. These Mandalas certainly function properly and control all prevailing power of evil spirits and put them away from the house. As these Mandalas have no bad impact, persons should not be in worry about harm as a return of these Mandalas. Mandala for any facing single or double facing houses never damage the good things of the houses. Their main purpose is to protect persons and their houses from all acts of witches, wizards, ghosts, phantoms, skeleton like life, black spirits etc. when Mandalas will be hung at home person will find good symptoms as laughing, content success, physical and mental growth, gain of wealth understanding, confidence, co-operation, courage eagerness etc. among the members of the house. As the result, there are constant flow of joy and free movement being away from fear and terror of evil spirits and all kinds of harmful bad and black spirits.

EAST-SOUTH FACING HOUSE

Houses of East-South facing need two Mandalas to hang to make houses free from all kinds of evil and black harmful spirits. Mankala for East facing houses and Mandala for South facing houses both should be hung systematically that means Mandala for East facing is for East side and another Mandala for South facing should be for south side of the double facing houses.

In such type of double facing houses persons should no

bear lot of trouble and pain from evil spirits and black spitits. In the morning and in the day time such houses will be calm and quite no disturbances from bad and harmful spirits. But at night evil and other kinds of black spirits occasionally appear and time to time fall upon human body to make persons suffer unexpectedly. In such houses too witches/wizards, ghosts, other black spirits, various unnatural fantoms etc. enter and move within four walls of the house causing horror, pain, problems and anxiety. Difficulties can't be solved easily. As evil spirits and other harmful spirits like to destroy human peace they create various problems and damage healthy and wealth of the persons. But the best and the easiest way to get rid of such problems persons should hang Mandalas according to the rule following all required limitations and conditions. Two Mandalas for East and South when hung in the homes of East-South facing properly being in rules given to be followed it is certain pain and anxiety vanish and there will be rays of happiness spread in the house. Persons should not have more fear in the mind and houses will be full of joy. No member of such houses should lament again being victim to any kinds of evil and harmful beings. Belief of persons in hanging tantric Mandalas at home is the wise step to move to smoothness. Instead of pain they will get gain in every turning of normal life. Again to cure unknown and undiagnosed diseases hanging Mandala according to rule of tantrism is the best way to end winter for spring season in human life. But it is a fun for men of science and do not believe in such concept. But I advise men of science that both Religion and science are equally important things to lead life successfully on the soil.

WEST-SOUTH FACING HOUSE

In every two facing house two Mandalas are essential to be used for the safety of persons in the house. In case of west-south facing houses a Mandala for west facing house should be hung to West side of the house and another Mandala of south facing house should be hung to south side of the house, when these two types of Mandalas are properly hung it is sure these types of houses will be quite free from the attack of harmful evil and black spirits. Persons can easily, get relief from such spirits. When Mandalas will be hung in the house evil spirits of all kinds will be away from the house. Any kinds of bad and black spirit can't fall upon human body. West-South facing houses mostly suffer from evil and black spirits. Such harmful spirits enter in such houses from window with flow of hard wind. They enter in the house and at night they would be active in creating horror, pain and problem for the persons of the house. Persons dwelling in such houses lose peace in mine and also suffer from unknown diseases. Physically weak persons-women and children became victim to such bad and harmful spirits. Such weak persons weep, shout, thrill etc. time to time. Unnatural fever, indigestion, vomiting, unnatural behaviours, abnormal looking, fasting for days, abnormal eating and drinking, high slumber, loss of slumber etc. are symptoms of use of power by evil spitits. All persons do not believe in such fact. The fact about such evil spirits and black spirits are dreamy fact for those who have not experienced it personally. But whatever the people of scientific attitude think many people suffer from abnormal evil spirits and many persons have tasted lot of pain and problems from such spirits. Those who have experienced and have borne high suppression from such spirits they would be quite straight forward to the tantric remedy without delaying a minute. Persons having such experience, I am sure, will agree my tantric doctrine and will be ready to follow my this atheistic tantrism. They will agree to hang the Mandala to get rid of pain and problems from unknown diseases caused by evil, bad and black harmful spirits. So I advise the persons of west and south facing house that they should not move in rumour and should not do this and that rather they have to hang the Mandalas to be free from all sorts of invisible, partly visible, dimly visible evil spirits and black spirits. Quick decision makes quick to recover the way to relief, happiness and success in life. Put fear, tear, confusion aside or out from the mind soon and step to the path of joy and delight to lengthen existence of valuable human life.

Four kinds of single Mandalas and four kinds of double

Mandalas are described for different single facing houses and double facing houses with a view to make know the people the importance of the tantric Mandalas. Function and values of Mandalas are really great to flow perennial joy and relief in human life.

INSTALLATION OF MANDALA

Installation of the Mandala in the house is a very careful action to be done. If Mandala is not installed properly and correctly, it does not function in full swing or it affects negatively. If any mistake is there in the installation of Mandala there and then it should be checked to correct the mistake. Here are some procedures to fix Mandala on the wall of the room of the house. The following are the procedures *(a)* The best day to hang the Mandala is Saturday. The alternative day is Tuesday *(b)* The right time to hang the Mandala is 7 o'clock at night *(c)* Two rods should be connected with the Mandala one is iron rod and another is copper rod *(d)* A guard pot is essential to be placed on the ground floor of the house *(e)* Iron rod is to be placed or erected at the top of the house *(f)* Copper rod is erected in the guard pot *(g)* The black thread of seven or twenty one or forty nine folded according to the condition of the house is prepared to be used *(h)* The length of the black thread is as long as the height of the house *(i)* the black thread is lined and must be properly tightened in a knot in seven points of the black thread is used to connect Iron rod at the top of the house with copper rod of the guard pot. *(k)* The guard pot contains seven elements. Those elements are (1) Ash (2) Crow's feather (3) Black soyabeam (4) fish bone (5) sand (6) char coal (7) soil. How to use those elements in the guard pot are clearly shown in the picture. *(l)* Length of rods and nails must be 49 inches (iron rod) 21 inches (copper rod) and one inch (nail) *(m)* The guard pot must be earthen pot after putting all seven elements in the guard pot systemically the pot must be put to the left side of the main gate of the house for both north facing and south facing house. It must be put to the right side of the main gate for the East facing house and the west facing house. If the required

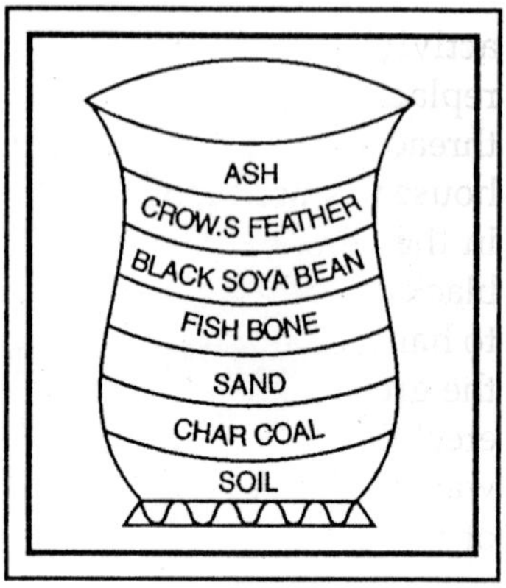

seven elements for the guard pot are not in order as shown in the figure it does not generate the power to fight with evil spirits, to put them out of the house and to check the new in coming such harmful spirits. One thing more to be known in time of installation of the guard pot is three raw bricks must be laid in triangular way and the pot must be put over those bricks as shown above. A copper rod is essential to stick at the centre of the pot. The length of the rod is twenty one inches. The height of the rod is twenty one inches. The height of the pot must be fifteen inches. When the copper rod is installed in the centre of the pot it will be 6 inches above the pot as shown in the picture. After completion of the guard pot this pot is connected with the Mandala with help of folded black thread. 49 folded black thread is very powerful folded thread. The middle one is 21 folded thread and 7 folded black thread is the least powerful one and is used for normal cases. First 7 folded black thread is used for 7 days and regular watch should be done in the household atmospheric motion, evil spirits influence upon the members of the house, if found positive effect the seven folded thread is fit and should be kept. If there is no positive effect 7 folded thread should be replaced by 21 folded thread. But in major cases that means high power of evil spirit or black spirit is poured in the house and has been difficult to check the spirits from evil

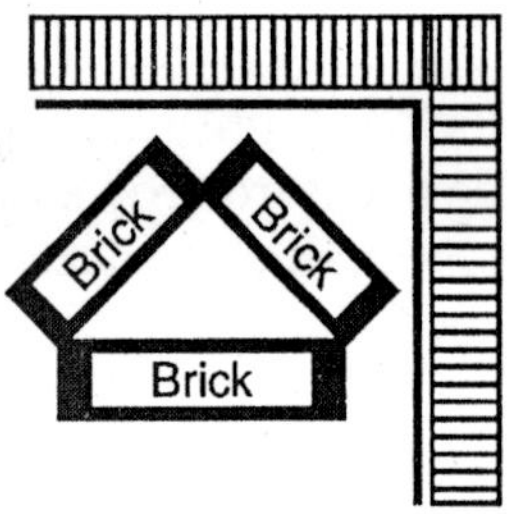

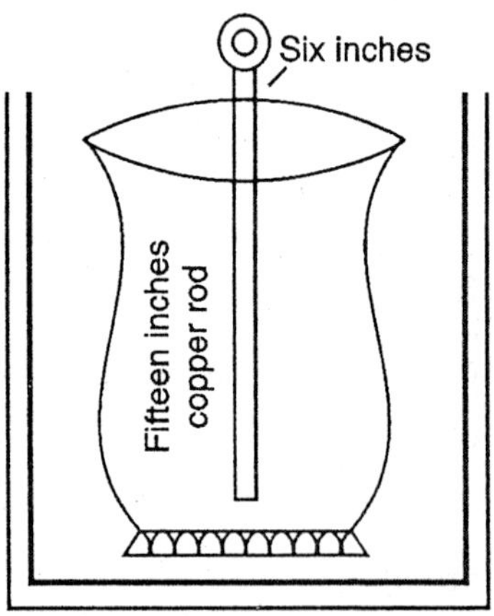

activities in this case 21 folded black thread also must be replaced by 49 folded black thread. In the use of 49 folded black thread whatever the power of those harmful spirits is in the house will be fully removed and their presence will be no where in the house. But in the very beginning the 49 and 21 folded black thread should not be used. First of all the user of the house to hang Mandala and the floor or ground for the guard pot on the ground floor of the house he/she or they must manage to erect the iron rod of 49 inches. This rod must be erected in this way as shown in the picture. In the iron rod erected at the top of the house the folded black thread is joined or connected according to the need of the house to be used to control evil spirits and all kinds of black spirits. The length of the folded black thread to cover the whole process of the installation of the Mandala depends upon the height of the house. From top to bottom of the house if it is 60 feet more than 60 feet folded black thread is need to cover all turnings of the house. For complete installation of the Mandala one side of the thread is knotted at the iron rod erected at the top of the house and another side is knotted at the copper rod of the guard pot. The folded blacks thread should be passed through the Mandala as shown in the picture. In the folded black thread 7 nails also must be knotted from iron rod to copper rod in the distance of about 3 to 7 feet. Prior to use the nails they are heated red so that they should not be in raw state. After completion of installation of Mandala in a passing of 7 hours it functions in full swing for the welfare of the members of the house. It helps to make persons of the house free from all sorts of pain and problems caused by all types of harmful evil and black spirits. The bad and black spirits which used to appear off and on in the houses specially sun lightless houses that are also brick built using soil as

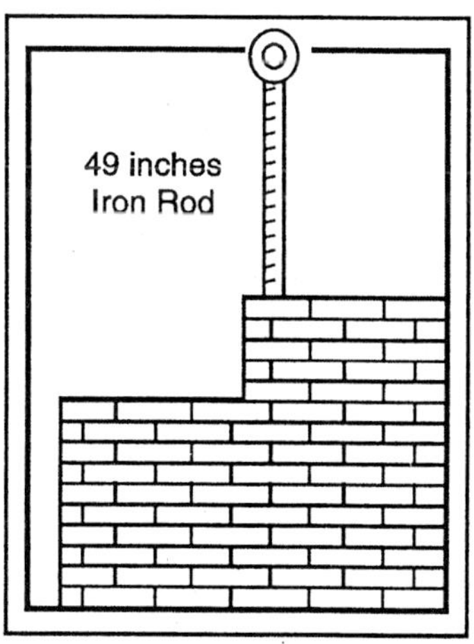

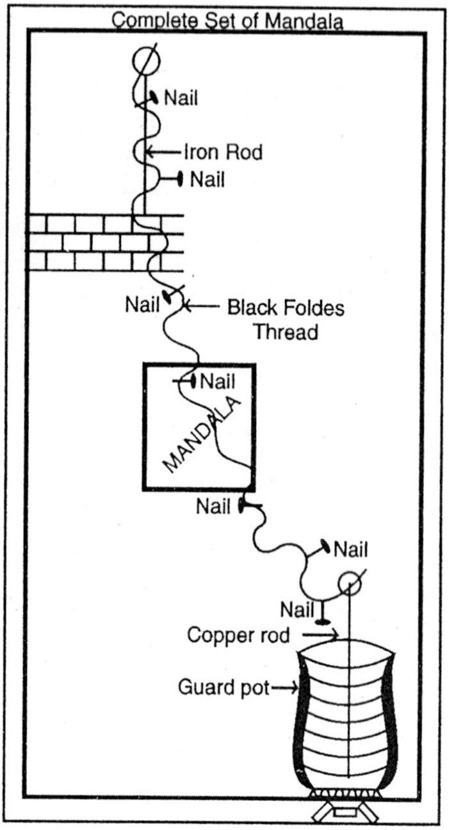

joint gum run away or vanish soon in the installation of complete set of Mandala. The abstract advantageous of the Mandala are (1) It increases spiritual strength in person (2) Quick recovery of sound health (3) Sound atmospheric development for co-operation and harmony among the member of the house. (4) No tears in eyes and no fear in mind (5) belief in superstition is replaced by reality. These five advantages are quick achievable advantages of the Mandala. Except these, there are many other benefits can be found in it in the long run and persons can easily be happy in the installation of Mandala at home or in any other place according to their need. As the spell-folded black thread itself is an active power generating thing against evil, bad and black spirits certainly the Mandala is more powerful when it is backed by such thread. So a separate chapter is allocated to narrate the importance of the black thread. This black thread when it is spelled and used in human body it protects persons from the attack of evil spirits and all kinds of harmful back spirits when they are out of their house. The invisible harmful spirits can be roaming everywhere in the air, dim sun light, darkness, rain, hot and chilled atmosphere and attack people accidentally. They can be quite safe from such attack of various kinds of evil and harmful black spirits in the use of the spelled folded black thread. These various types of evil and black spirits are just like virus mentioned in the medical science may fall on human body even in minor mistake in their movement in the universal space. In Nepal all most all rural parts of the country are suffering from such virus like evil spirits and harmful black spirits. Mostly people of rural parts suffer from witches/wizards, ghosts, spirit of unnatural or immatured dead persons, other black spirits as Bhuta, Preta etc. In the remote area of Nepal because of illiteracy people believe in superstition. If persons become ill they think it is due to witch/wizard. Nepal is a country full of villages. Those villages are not developed villages. There in the villages majority of people are farmers. They are economically weak and illiterate. Due to mixture of so many fantastic factors their thinking was poor and believed in such evil spirits and black spirits. So the evil beings and other such harmful beings empowered over the people and rooted strongly and deeply in their mind unavoidable and lasted for ever since centuries. These types of bad spirits are strongly existing and has been a Himalayan task for the people to be free from their dirty and harmful games. More effort is spent more such harmful spirits began to linger in human community. So solution for such problems has been more complicated for the people. The dilemma dropped in all Nepalese dwellings and in most of Hindus dwellings. So evil spirits attack is harder than hard diseases. Since ancient time curing of such problem of painful diseases scattered. As evil being has been quite religious deductive method worshipping the gods and goddesses of power was the best method. It was hoped by the sufferers that they would be free from suffering when gods and goddesses are pleased by human offerings. This was the way of treatment in old religion. But unlike this old method my way of treatment is installation of Mandala at home and use of spelled black folded thread in the human body. This method of curing never encourage the people to surrender their life to gods and goddesses. The old method of tantrism for treatment is solely based on atheistic tantrism where as my new method based on semi atheistic tantrism. Most of the things that are used in my tantric treatment for healing is unknown wonderful as well as mysterious and are different from things used in old method. Mandala, the black thread and some other ordinary things which are available things used in this semi atheistic tantric method. As the black thread plays vital role in the treatment of unknown diseases caused by evil spirits and all kinds of harmful black spitits I have presented about it in detail in the separate chapter.

INGREDIENTS OF GUARD POT

In the guard pot there seven elements play vital role to generate the power through the black folded thread. Among those seven elements ASH is one of the ingredients that is put on the top layer of the guard pot. Why is ASH on the top of the power or guard pot? This thing has power to wash away the harmful quality of other things. So ASH can wash away the strength of the evil beings and harmful black beings and make them weak in power. As the time passes on without any break in the use of power generated by the guard pot all kinds of evil spirits resistance become weak. At last such spirits have to run away from their working station or place. Another role played by ASH is this thing is quite dry by product of wood and coal. No living likes to eat it because of its tastelessness. When evil spirits see ASH they also try to go somewhere to be away from Ash. It is ASH which is used by Shadu, Santa, hermits etc. Who have denounced the family and society and who have no hope of any kinds of material things to enjoy. They also have given up human love kindness and sympathy in life. Again ASH is a purified thing which adds peace in mind of the people. So ASH is used at the top Level of the guard pot.

Another ingredient used in the guard pot in the second top level is the crow's feather. This feather also has played high role in the guard pot to fight against the evil and harmful black spirits. A crow is a black bird and supposed as one of the clever and sensitive birds that can know the appearance of harmful evil beings and make people to be responsive to its crying. It carries the message of arrival of evil elements in the people's dwelling. Evil and all kinds of black spirits are afraid of the crow. They hide their head from the crow. So the crow's feather is useful thing in the guard pot to make it powerful to struggle with all kinds of harmful elements. One thing about the wonder of this feather is witches/wizards, ghosts and many other fantoms do not like this feather. So evil beings run away from the crow's feather. But only selected feather should be used to put in the guard pot. The first matured feather of the wing must be used for this purpose. If not available the first matured feather second one and if the second one also is not available the third, fourth or fifth must be put in the pot. But the other feather as the second, the third, the fourth and the fifth feather will not be as powerful as the first feather. According to its rank the power of it also will be lesser than the previous one. Crow, the Hindu religion says is an incarnation of Yama (the gods of death). So people would worship the crow to please it. This concept is to some extent right. In fact, the crow is a very careful, useful and intelligent black bird. It can know the nature and behaviour of the people. If it sees any evil persons and black spirits it will watch them continuously until it finds out the reason behind their movement. So the crow's feather is taken to use it in the guard pot as second powerful ingredient to generate power to fight with evil spirits. This feather is also equally important to be used in another way to protect the persons from the attack of the various harmful beings. Another importance of this feather is if persons are going to some place with same unknown persons at that time all of sudden if any harmful beings intended to fall upon them with a view to create pain and problems, they can't harm them if they had the crow's feather in their body. So it is advised that persons who have to move to doubtful and fearful places of harmful spirits go with this feather. But put it in the body in hidden ways unseen by other.

Black soyabean is another equally useful and powerful thing. So it is taken as third important ingredient to be used in the guard pot. This beam has unique power which plays great role to save the people from bad and black evil spirits. This bean is such bean which can't be destroyed or consumed by any insect. It can't be eaten by any harmful evil spirits. When any bad and harmful spirits see this bean they live away from it. This is special power of the black bean to check evil beings. Any evil beings do not like this beam and they take this bean as poison. It is so because of its black colour cover. If the black coloured cover of the bean is removed or put off it will be of no power can be consumed by the insects and can be ineffective to evil spirits. Three coloured soyabeans are found. White soyabean, brown soyabean and black soyabean. White soyabean is used by persons of bad intention to create problems to other persons. Brown soyabean is of common one is used by common persons to gain protein and the black soyabean is used to put away harmful spirits. So this black soyabean is taken to add power to weaken the evil spirits and all sorts of trouble creating spirits. So it is a quite suitable ingredient to be used in the guard pot to generate more power. This bean is a common and simple thing of mysterious power to check and weaken all types of evil and harmful actions of the dangerous evil beings.

The fourth essential ingredient for the guard pot is the fish done. But this fish bone must be matured central fish bone to be fit for the pot which generates power in the pot. The fish bone is such ingredient for the pot which generates power in the pot to cause pain in the evil beings to make them repent for their evil steps and to make them realise they should not move further step to add more pain in human body. It is all known fact that fish is a watery creature supposed as a symbol of reward in getting success in action. Again fish is a mild creature with inward strength to fight with harmful living beings. As fishes are of many kinds with unknown capacity it is fit to overcome any sort of problems and obstacles on the way to forwarding. No evil and harmful black spirits can fall down upon human beings because of the help of fish bone's hidden capacity. The matured central bone of the fish is a hard flat cream coloured thing with several thorns on both sides. The both sided throngs are harmful to those who touch it without due care. So evil spirits also are afraid of this central fish bone. The incoming bad and evil spirits when they see this bone while moving here and there in the house they do not venture to stay there rather leave the house for being away from harm of the fish bone. They escape away from the pot and away from the house to be safe from all possible human fabrications on them. So it is said that the fish bone has its special quality to add strength in the guard pot to weaken evil spirit for the happy and tranquil atmosphere in the human dwelling. Another ingredient which is the fifth element of the guard pot is sand. Sand is such ingredient of the pot that is dry and tasteless. This sand plays a role of making the bad and evil spirits as well as all kinds of harmful black spirits lean and thin. It is the sand that produces dry atmosphere in the house and make difficult to exist evil spirits and other various bad spirits there. When such various spirits enter in the house with a view to create disturbance in the house by scattering pain and problems in human body they themselves become weak and passive because of the unhealthy influence of the sand. Effect of the guard pot if they intend to linger in the house being invisible and sometimes being visible in the dark night falls upon them. Those spirits, at last, are defected and go away from the house where the guard pot is installed. Among the seven ingredient of the guard pot all are natural things. Some are black in colour and some are white and dark brown. Again some are creamy and ashy in colour. Sand is dim white ingredient which slowly makes realises or feels evil spirits and black spirits that their black activities can't harm the people for long time and they feel that their such acts should be given up. Such kind of change in the evil spirits is real contribution of sand. So it is very important ingredient of the guard pot. This white colour of the sand is the main seed to grow good feeling in bad and evil things or evil beings. This is the special power and quality of the sand. It is sand that saturates evil power or harmful evil beings and it dries the bad power. It replaces white and good power in place of bad one. So this fifth ingredient of the pot has its speciality and is equally useful as other ingredient to put the pot in action smoothly. So the intrinsic or real value of sand is greater than its face value for the guard pot.

The other ingredient that is sixth element of the pot is char coal. It can be put in the pot. In two different ways *(a)* In piece and *(b)* In the form of power. Charcoal is dark black thing. It acts to decrease the power of black spirits. This element also has possessed wonderful power to minimise and to eliminate harmful evil power of these evil beings. This thing acts slowly and mildly in the beginning and hardly in the end. All know it that charcoal also is a dry thing. It has wonderfully ugly taste. This element also is not liked by those destructive beings. If a piece of char coal or powder of it is thrown upon the body of harmful evil elements it plays negative impact upon them. Such spirits will be discouraged, they will be frail and they will be upset due to lack of potentiality to apply their power in creating destruction of human happiness. It is charcoal that provides bright ray in the human dwelling by putting away all types of harms and danger from those evil spitits. All those abnormal trouble creating elements disappear from the house of the people. So this black thing is vitally important for the guard pot. White and bright ray of this black element is a unique quality of the charcoal.

The last but the most valuable ingredient of the guard pot is soil. Soil is the inside base of the power generating pot. Nothing will be useful and valuable in the world unless it is visibly laid on soil. In the guard pot it is soil on which other six different ingredients are laid linking each other to generate human welfare power and strength. Getting support of soil other all factors of the pot function all the time to prevent harmful elements that venture to turn the human happiness into misery. As soil is the inside base support of the guard pot all other ingredients generate helpful power for human beings. Without soil in the pot no action will be done effectively by this tantric pot. Similarly no living beings whether they are normal, good and gentle or abnormal, evil and harmful exist on the earth without soil. So every moment all kinds of evil, bad and harmful spirits move here and these on soil with trouble creating desire in the life of human beings. At the same time human beings also are moving to be safe from the attack of such spirits. People use many remedies to make such attack of evil beings null and void. In this way there is hide and seek between normal people and evil and harmful spirits. Evil spirits roam human door to door in search of human beings to flow pain and problem in them. Human beings also apply various tantric means to be safe from them. In such antagonistic competition between human beings and evil as well as devil spirits time to time simple, gentle and mild nature human beings become victim to evil and harmful black spirits. Such people suffer much physically and mentally in the running of the normal life on the Earth. Soil is the last ingredient used on the base of the guard pot influences harmful and evil spirit constantly for peace and happiness of human beings. It will combat with all evil spirits continuously so those spirits will be weak and escape form the human dwellings.

So it is my sincere advice to those who are suffering from unknown diseases caused by evil spirits and all kinds of harmful black spirit to erect or install this wonderful and powerful soil based guard pot to get rid of mysterious suffering. Soil is the base element of this power generating pot because nothing is possible in the world without soil. Another reason of being soil as basic element of the pot is soil is coherent element which has productive power. Other things can produce other things only when there is soil on the base. On soil people according to their need can grow various movable and unmovable things. So in the guard pot it makes move all those six ingredients active to produce protective power for persons to be safe from the attack of all kinds of evil and harmful beings. Again it moves to remove all evil strength picking up it from the house and place and close all points of entrance of the house to put all evil power of evil beings away from the house for ever.

This is the short narration of seven ingredients contained in the guard pot. All those ingredients are equally important to generate antipower for all evil beings. This pot is the centre of power which regularly functions to mitigate all types of strength and power of the evil beings. All those seven elements of the pot have their own speciality that produce quite different vitality to generate the original quality to be fit to combat with all pain and problem creators in human beings life. So it is sure that power of the guard pot without any trace of doubt erect to enjoy benefit of it to be free from all kinds of troubles and miseries though it is unseen immeasurable, unknown and undiagnosed in colour and symptoms.

Now closing this chapter about the guard pot I have

intended to draw attention of the people to other essential elements of the tantrism. Those essential elements are *(a)* Rudrakshya *(b)* Patal of rose flower *(c)* Jasmine flower *(d)* Black seed of Ritha *(e)* Raw rice *(f)* Leaf of Bar and Pipal *(g)* Bone and skin.

(A) Rudrakshya : In this tantrism Rudrakshya is a bit wild but holy bean like thing. It is quite useful thing which helps to be free from the attack of evil and black spirits. In Hindu religion also this wild holy fruit is used as a very useful and powerful thing. It is said that this wild bean like wild fruit has possessed divine power and used by hermits, sages and monks as gods and goddesses favourite thing. Great gods and goddesses of power of Hindu religion like Lord Shiva, Lord krishna, Lord Ram chandra, goddess Parvati, goddess Durga goddess Sita etc. have liked to use it as garland. Hindu religion says that Rudrakshya works as life guard on the one hand and a means to get chance to enter in the heaven on the other. There is more about this wild holy fruit in tantrism. The Rudrakshya is taken as a means of protection of life from evil spirits and other bad and black beings. It is taken as a mean of medicine in the tantrism. When persons put Rudrakshya in water for seven minutes and drink the water abnormality caused by evil beings and other kinds of harmful bad and black beings can be relieved in short periods. Another way of its use is to hang it on the neck, on the arm or on the wrist stringing it on seven folded black thread. But prior to use it for remedial purpose it should be spelled to empower it against evil and other harmful spirits. This is the uncommon and unique beauty of this bean Rudrakshya. In fact Rudrakshya is a multipurpose bean used in different walks of human life. Hermits and sages use it as virtuous fruit which saves persons to commit or do harm. From wrong doers. The feeling of person's wrong doing also can be checked by use of this wild and holy fruit bean.

Rose petal also is taken as another important thing in this tantrism, Rose petal is holy thing which helps persons when they have some disorder, dejection random thinking and feeling, lack of self-confidence, fear etc. Rose is a beautiful and attractive flower. This flower is found in many colour with sweet scent some are found without scent. I have taken rose as a panacea like thing to cure known and unknown diseases to medical science. How to use and which colour should be used depends upon the nature of disease. There are mainly red white yellow, pink, purple etc. Persons who cry loudly and bite other persons in anger without any clear reason. It must be known that they must be highly influenced and guided by bad and black spirits or evil spirits. For such kind of disease red rose is useful to those persons to cure. Again persons who without any reason keep silent and do not want to speak with other persons and like to stay in a place. In appearance of such symptom in persons is also a cause of influence of bad elements or evil spirits. White rose is useful to cure such kind of disease. Persons who want to abandon the house being in abnormal emotion and time to time get ready to go out and away from the house is another symptom of influence upon them by the evil spirits and black spirits. Such persons of abnormal nature may vanish from the family if they are not checked and taken great care by other family members. This kinds of disease is very dangerous though it seem to be simple. Such diseased persons should not be kept alone in the house or any place. So they must be taken great care all the time by concerned persons. For such disease yellow coloured rose is useful to use in curing.

Persons suffering from unknown disease and because of such disease they cry and talk to themselves unclearly must be influenced by evil spirits or harmful black spirits. Such persons can be cured with the help of pink coloured rose. Their crying and talking to themselves is void and no reason. Such diseased persons sometimes weep bitterly expressing their discontent of not caring and loving them by other members of the family. Such persons being abnormal state create quarrel in the house. But in case of mixed symptom of unknown disease in persons purple coloured rose is considered as the best rose. Mixed symptom means the symptom which belong to symptoms that need red, white, yellow or pink roses to cure the disease. If all coloured roses are used to cure the disease of mixed symptoms that also can't be proper way. So for such mixed symptom in the diseases purple rose is considered as the best roses for curing.

This is all the use of various coloured roses for various symptoms of the diseases. Persons should know clearly about it and should be careful to use different coloured roses in different diseases.

Now another important thing to be known is how to use the rose for curing the diseases. The proper and correct use of the rose for positive effect on the disease are as following.

- *(a)* Rose should not be plucked from the plant
- *(b)* Single rose should not be used rather the petals of the rose should be used.
- *(c)* When petals of the rose is taken out from the rose they should not be put on the ground.
- *(d)* Only seven petals of the rose are enough for the treatment.
- *(e)* All seven petals of the rose should be dropped or put in a glass of pure water
- *(f)* The time of the dropping those petals of rose should be exactly seven o'clock in the morning and duration must be forty nine minutes.
- *(g)* The suitable day for the preparation of this rose medicine is Saturday. The alternative day is Tuesday.

The above given seven conditions or limitations should be strictly fulfilled in the use of the rose for curing the unknown and mysterious disease caused by evil spirits and black spirits.

Another important flower used as essential thing to cure the unknown diseased by evil beings is Jasmine. This flower is used to cure only for children. When children of various age suffer all of sudden due to wicked action of the evil spirits and other harmful black spirits such as witches/wizards, ghost, fantoms of various shape and size with various evil capacities etc. can be cured by using Jasmine. Children of one to five years old if suffer from any sorts of evil or black spirits three Jasmine flowers should be used for curing. Children from six to twelve years old need seven Jasmine flowers to cure. How to use the flower? In a glass of fresh drinking water Jasmine flowers should be dropped or put at seven o'clock in the morning. The flowers must be plucked from the plant and there and then they should the dropped in water. The minimum time to put Jasmine flowers in water is forty nine minutes. The flowers can be put more time and more days in the water. It does not harm though the flowers are put in water. The use of such water should be done very strictly. Seven tea spoonful water should be drunk by the patient once or twice a day. The exact time to drink such holy medicine water is seven in the morning and at night. If it is used once a day it should be at night. This water must be used for seven days continuously. If there has been break in the use of water it must be reused continuously from one to seven days. One who uses this medicine water must think about its impact very critically to find out change or recovery after the application of this water. If there is slight recovery this water should be used more than seven days. More days means twenty one days. If seven days are enough use of it must be stopped. But one thing more about the use of this water is use twice a day is better or more effective than once a day for quick recovery. This is all about how to use Jasmine flower in the treatment for the unknown diseases.

Another essential thing to use in this tantrism as medicine for the unknown and undiagnosed diseases is the black seed of Ritha. When the persons all of sudden without any clear reason or symptoms suffer this black seed can be used in the treatment. But this thing is only for external use. If people feel pain in any part of body take seven seeds of Ritha, bind all seeds in a piece of black cloth, give holy smoke of insane (Dhupa) then put it on the pained part of the body for several times continuously. The duration must be seven minutes or more than that. People get relief from pain. If the pain reoccurred the same process should be repeated until complete relief. The black seed of Ritha is useful for all kinds of pain. It is useful for all patients who are victim to evil spirits and harmful black spirits.

Raw rice is another useful thing to be used to be away from the painful effect of evil and black spirits when the people fall into inhuman attack of the evil spirits and the black spirits. Influence of such attack can be removed by the use of raw rice How to use raw rice? Take a handful of raw rice. Make it wet. Give holy smoke of insane (Dhupa). Go top floor of the house.

Throw or scatter a little to East direction, a little to North direction and a little to South direction. Then throw a little to the sky and a little to the Earth (Ground). Make it a little remain. Put the remaining little on the head of the patients. The remaining should not be put or fallen on the floor or on the ground. Again take seven raw rice grains from the remaining. Give one grain to the patient to eat. Swallow it with water. It should not be chewed. Seven grains of rice should be eaten every day for 7 days. The right time to eat the grain of rice is 7 o'clock at night. This grain of raw rice is quite useful and helpful to cure unknown disease specially the accidental and unpredictable diseases caused by evil spirits and black spirits.

The next or sixth essential thing is leaf of Bar and Pipal. This leaf of Bar and Pipal helps to heal the disease caused by harmful evil and black spirits. In Hindu religion the tree of Bar and Pipal are regarded twin god and goddess. By worshipping these both trees people can be free from all kinds of pain and problems. They will be saved from the merciless attack of the evil spirits and black spirits. So every Hindus worships these both trees with view that they will be free from hard days. Any anxiety and trouble would not fall upon them and life will be quite and easy. But in this tantrism leaves of the both Bar and Pipal trees are used differently. Seven leaves of Bar must be binded with black thread. The binding should be completed with seven turnings. Seven leaves of Pipal also must be binded with black thread. Here also the binding should be finished with seven turnings. Put these binded leaves in the pure water for one to three hours. Put a piece of char coal in the water pot. Give holy smoke of insane (Dhup). But do not put the pot on the floor or on the ground. Sprinkle the water with the help of binded Bar from main gate of the house to all over the house. Secondly the same process should be done through the binded leaves of Pipal. Put the dipped leaves pot on the table or some other place which is three or more feet above the floor or the ground. This sprinkling of water should be repeated. Once at 7 o'clock in the morning every day regularly for 7 days. If there is sick person in the house. This water is drinkable for all person. Seven tea spoonful of water should be drunk. One tea spoonful of water for one time. This process of drinking water is applicable for the normal disease. It the disease is severe one twice a day or thrice a day should be given to drink to the patient. This is a brief narration of Bar and ripal. It is clear that leaf of these trees help to check the evil and harmful influence of evil and black spirits.

The other essential thing to check evil spirits and black spirits is Bone. Any bone of any animal can be taken to use for the purpose. But only thing that should be thought of is the bone either should be of legs or it should be of hands of the animal. Wild animal's bone is more powerful than the bone of domesticated animals. Tiger's bone is the most powerful bone. If the tiger's bone is available no other bone should be used. It is the best bone. Any other bone can't be alternative to it. How to use bone for tantric purpose? This is the main thing to be explained clearly to make know the common people so that they also could be able to use it in needful moment. First of all the person who is going to use bone as a means of protection he/she must be sure which bone it is wild animals's bone or bone of the domesticated animal's if the person had hard case the wild animal's bone should be used if possible the tiger's bone should be used. Tiger, we all know it is a hard wild and merciless animal. It is as cruel and hard as evil spirits and black spirits. Eye for eye and tooth for tooth this principle is used here for the treatment of hard cases. But use of the bone of the domesticated animals can not be exactly similar to nature of pain and problems caused by the harmful spirits. In the use of the bone of the domesticated animal recovery from the disease takes more time. So for the quick recovery wild animal's bone should be used if possible the tiger's.

The method of using the bone of the animals is here. Take the bone of hands or legs of the animal. Bind it with the black thread. The binding should be of seven round binding. Put the bone in a piece of black cloth pack it in the cloth. Give smoke of insane (Dhupa) put the spelled bone at the top of the house at 7 o'clock at night. Press it with a brick or stone. Leave it there for whole night. Take the bone next day. If somebody suffers in the house the bone should be put in the middle part of the body of the sufferer in a hidden way. It is better to put the bone behind in the middle part of body close to backbone. The sufferer feels relief soon from suffering. This bone also should not be put on the ground. If it falls on the ground or put on the floor by mistake it must be prepared again following all rules given to be done. This is all about the preparation and use of the spelled bone to protect persons from pain and problems caused by evil spirits and harmful bad and black spirits. Application of all these things from Rudrakshya to bone or skin help people to heal diseases and trouble for short period. When there is problem or pain in life is solved the duration of means also finish. But for permanent cure every body must erect Mandala at home. One thing I want to write here is in this tantrism the most important thing the person should have is belief to apply any method of this tantrism. So I advise to trust it and enjoy a lot from the tantrism.

THE BLACK THREAD

The thread which I am going to describe is a thread of tantric power. It is none but the black thread. This is the tantric thread that helps the people to get rid of evil spirits and all kinds of bad harmful and black spirits. But the ordinary black thread does not help the people to solve their problem. This thread will be useful and powerful when the required ritual spell is poured in it. But thread of other colour can't be useful to solve the problem caused by such harmful spirits. The power spread by abnormal harmful spirit in every nook and corner of the house can be checked only by the use of the spelled black thread. This is a magic thread and it has tantric power to make evil power and black power null and void. This is the thread used to heal unknown diseases and invisible disease like events that can't be cured by any expert physicians by using all kinds well known modern medicines and by using all kinds of medical apparatus. This thread is a unique remedy, a panacea specially for the patients who are suffering from evil spirts like witches wizards, ghosts, mental disturbances caused by unnatural beings and abnormal beings, impact of ill or misspell of the priests and other various illusions, fantoms, cowardness due to physical weakness, abnormality because of the influence of superbeings such as monks, hermits, sages etc. It is also useful for those persons who time to time cry being in abnormal state, weep all of sudden without any reason, loss of slumber, walking in somnambulistic state etc. This thread can easily be used in many other abstract cases too to be free from them. But the raw thread can't provide any benefits as mentioned above as sweet fruit of the spelled thread. The black thread is prepared under strict rules pouring ritual and tantric abstract spells in it. So the black thread will be a powerful thread only when it is made following all abstract tantric spells and can be used as a powerful means to cure the unknown and unseen diseases. The spelled thread is categorized into three groups or types *(a)* Seven folded black thread *(b)* twenty one folded black thread and *(c)* fortynine folded black thread. For seven folded black thread it needs seven days to prepare similarly twenty one days for twenty one folded back thread and forty nine days for forty nine folded black thread. The use of the black thread depends upon the nature of the case or disease. In case of light and primary cases seven folded black thread is used. If the case is of a bit harder or serious twenty one folded black thread is used. Only in major old cases or diseases forty nine bold at black thread is used. As this thread is very useful for the safety of human body from the evil spirits and all kinds of harmful bad and black spirits it is equally important and useful for the protection of residence and occupational centres. Here may arises a question about why the black thread is the only thread to use for the purpose of controlling, curing, putting people and dwelling places free from the attack of evil spirits and why not other coloured thread be used to meet the same purpose. The answer for this question is every colour represents its own significance with various quality. White colour is symbol of peace. Red is sign of revolution, yellow represents denunciation or abundance of materialistic happiness. Blue colour is for purity. These all colours could not check the black and evil deeds of evil spirits and black spirits. Black and harmful activities of the bad persons such as witches wizards can be checked by the spelled black thread to control and to put away all harms of evil beings and black beings. To solve any black deeds of the black beings people most use the black things. So the black thread, black feather, black bean etc. are taken to be used to get rid of black and evil things. So this black thread is used to reach to success in combat with evil and harmful spirits with a view to make the people happy by taking them away from such spirits. It also I assure those who are suffering from the unknown and undiagnosed diseases that this spelled black thread is helpful for them to be free from such diseases. I am sure this spelled black thread has unique power. It can early defeat those evil beings and black beings. People will be protected from the attack of all sorts of harms that are sent by harmful spirits when this powerful thread will be used by the people no bad and black spirits can enter, dominate, infuse harmful effect upon human body and also in the dwelling places of human beings. This is the super and wonderful power quality of the black thread. This thread unlike caste and creed can be possessed to use by all persons. But the only great thing required to use it is the patient or any common people should have faith in it when it is taken to use it. Trust first then treatment, this is the best way to healing of any diseases.

Though this thread seems to be simple thing outwardly it is weighty inwardly and its application is not easy. It has certain conditions and limitations to be fulfilled for its application to get its positive impact upon the concerned person and place. The conditions and limitations are clearly described below so that even a layman could understand it and become able to apply it when he/she will be in unfavourable situation and he/she is in need of the magic medicine black thread to use for getting relief.

Conditions and limitations :

(a) The black thread prepared in ritual and tantric spell should not be used for blind, dumb, deaf persons if they are so by birth.

(b) The black thread should not be put off from the body or taken out from the place except in the mentioned period.

(c) Proper method as guided by the concerned person about its use must be maintained

(*d*) Any given things by anybody that belong to gods and goddesses should not be used

(*e*) Guided or given duty to be done regularly by the patient or user of the thread

(*f*) Malhandling of the thread may cause negative impact on the patient or user.

(*g*) Ritual performance of Gods and goddesses should not be done using the thread on the body.

(*h*) Thread of other colour similar to black thread should not used or replaced for the same purpose.

(*i*) Thread given for a particular person should not be used by other persons.

(*j*) Thread should not be fallen down on the floor or on the ground.

(*k*) Backing materials used for this thread must be maintained properly.

He/she must be very careful and attentive to all these conditions and limitations for effective application of this remedial tantric thread.

Preparation of this powerful remedial thread is a difficult task. It needs many things and takes many days. To prepare this thread the minimum days required is seven days and the maximum days is fourty nine days. In time of preparation of this wonderful and powerful black thread all required things being in strict rules and regulations should be used. Meditation for hours and days according to the nature of disease, also should be done to flow anti current or anti waves of all kinds against the power of evil spirits and black spirits in the thread to heal the pain and suffering of the patients and flow of anti current in the thread to heal the pain and suffering of the patients. Flow of anti current or anti waves in the thread to check all evil beings, power is the most important but very difficult task in the preparation of this tantric black thread. But the preparation of this remedial thread is a remarkable beauty of this tantrism.

For the preparation of this tantric black thread here is special day. The quite suitable day is Saturday. Another second important day is Tuesday. Use of this thread should be done in these two days. But the preference should be given to Saturday. Persons who want to use this thread must use two days. Saturday and Tuesday in a week must not be forgot by users. Time to use it also should be considered. The right time to use the black thread is seven o'clock at night. The second right time is seven o'clock in the morning. If this thread is used in any other time it may not be effective in the same capacity as it is used in the exactly mentioned time or it will be less effective to generate the power. The speciality and beauty of this thread is it does not give any other side effect in the health and body of the user. In case of misinterpretation about signs and symptoms of the diseases caused by evil and black spirits it will not work effectively or it does not work at all. Meditation is one of the most important parts of treatment of this system. No other tasks are needed to be done as in the medical treatment. Persons who are suffering from the disease should meditate as they are directed to do it. It is needed to do. Some have to meditate one time in a day and some have to do it twice or more than twice in a day. This system is a new application as tantric means to gear up the strength to push away influence of the evil spirits and all kinds of black spirits. It is found from the inquiry and research that majority of sufferers from harmful spirits are women of different ages and children. It is so because women and children are soft hearted persons. So they are easily attacked by such harmful spirits using sometimes the lightest and some times the hardest evil spell upon them. All kinds of evil spirits fall upon females and children in three different ways. *(a)* By offering food *(b)* By touching body and *(c)* By glancing at persons in a serious and mysterious way. Among these three the first one is very hard and affect the persons very seriously. To cure such diseases caused because of first way takes at least forty nine days or more than that. But in care of suffering from *(b)* and *(c)* Ways it will be easy to cure. In *(b)* and *(c)* Ways the time taken to care will be between seven to fortynine days. It may be seven days, it may be twenty one days or it may be forty nine days. It depends upon the nature of suffering or disease caused by evil spirits. The addition of more days in forty nine days is required in case of the hardest and extra ordinary old diseases.

But in usual cases the required days are between seven to forty nine days. Again it depends upon the folding of the black thread too. More the folding more will be its strength to fight with evil spirits. But this remedial black thread can be used for other purposes also. One worth of the thread worthy to be mentioned here is persons of weak health when feel uneasiness or weakness physically should use it. It helps them to generate required strength and makes them able to pass normal life again.

Apart form curing diseases caused by evil spirits and black spirits this thread is highly helpful for those persons who are issueless. If issueless persons use this thread in a strict conditional limitations it is possible to have issues for them. The conditional limitations are *(a)* Age limitation and *(b)* limitation of the couple's age are main things to be considered under the conditional limitation of *(a)* Age of the male person should be below fifty five *(b)* Male person should be twenty five years old in minimum *(c)* Age of the female persons should be below thirty five *(d)* Female person's age should be twenty or a few months older the conditional limitation of *(b)* (1) Age of male and female when combined should be eighty or below eighty years. (2) Age of male persons and female persons when combined should be forty in minimum. These are the conditional limitations of age bar to be maintained by the issueless couple to be effective in solution for the problems of issueless case.

The remedial black thread is a multi dimensional black thread. It has many good but no bad effect. It has many points of strength but no weakness and voidness. It has many solution but no problem. So the value of this black thread is very high in this tantrism and it is the main sting of this tantric system. The complete mechanism of my neo-tantrism consists of three things *(a)* The black thread *(b)* The Mandala and *(c)* Guard pot. When these three major elements are joined systematically the tantrism will be in full swing to put away, to fight and control all kinds of evil spirits and harmful black spirits.

It is the spelled folded black tantric thread to make linkage rod to rod means iron rod at the top of the house is linked with the copper rod of the guard pot of the ground of the house passing through the Mandala. It is the thread that flows anti evil strength to save the house and persons of the house. It is the tantric black thread that is used to bind evil spirits specially the witches & wizards, to put them in control, to punish them for their evil deed over human beings and to cast lot of pain and problems. It is the spelled black thread that provides hidden happiness in the life of the people. So interested persons who have faith in it is advised to use it for their natural benefit.

Unlike my this powerful black thread there are many other kinds of threads in use for different religions and tantric purposes in different name in Hindu religion as well as Buddhist religion. In fact thread is a simple thing in outward form. But it has high inward vigour which promises human beings to protect them from merciless happenings to provide them lasting life with peace, harmony and tauntingly. Those popular different kinds of threads used in Hindu religion and Buddhist religion are mainly categorised as (1) Jajanka (2) Pashuka (3) Kokha and (4) Janai. These name for the threads are used for human welfare. Jajanka and pashuka are used for ritual performances. Kokha and janai are used for the protection of human body. But all these four kinds of threads are raw threads. Some are white in colour and some are made of thread of different colour. But all these kinds are religious threads and have no negative effect.

FOUR MAJOR BASES OF THE TANTRISM

The four major bases of this tantrism are four truth. They are very old truth as old as the Earth herself. These truths are universally acceptable truths. They are (A) The sun (B) Air (C) Water and (D) Land. The creation of every thing of the universe are solely and wholely the combination of these four elements. In absence of one element among these four creation of any thing is impossible. Here on this Earth, are innumerable creation. Some are movable and some are immovable with their unique and original characteristics. In every creation there are benefits and harms. When the creation makes or takes motion and signal of their existence as living beings it is sure they produce things whether those things are good or bad for other living. Good things push other things or living forward to move with hope and desire but bad ones push other things or livings backward with various pains and problems that destroy and damage other creation. Here, in this tantrism, is talked only human beings, good and bad things brought continuously by human beings, creation to show how people are suffering from human beings themselves. In the vast oceanic creation of thousands billions of actions and reactions of their world this book specially deals with action oriented religious performance of the people which have been good sometimes for the people and bad sometimes for the people. Among many subjects, tantrism is such subject which is vast, vague, and mysterious one that can't be measured easily and authentically. But it helps persons to make them free from pains and problem sent for them by evil spirits and harmful black spirits. The taste of good tantrism is always sweet for the people and with the help of such tantrism people can be happy and prosperous. Sages, hermits, monks etc. getting super help from gods and goddesses of power provide persons good and sweet taste of tantrism and free them from cobweb of pain and problem. But on the other hand witches, wizards and many other kinds of evil spirits and black harmful spirits throw poison like evil thing on persons to draw them to trouble and miseries. This is bad and harmful tantrism. All evil spirits and black spirits also get mercy of the gods and goddesses of power and cast their evil power upon human life. So it is gods and goddesses of power that turn human fate to happiness and misery such gods and goddesses of power belong to Hindu religion and Buddhist religion. But my this book 'Tantrism in Nepal' is entirely different from old tantrism. It is already mentioned that my this book on tantrism is unlike old one reflects the new ways of solution for solving pain and problems caused by bad and evil spirits. As this tantrism wholly and solely has four major basic truths. Now I write more about these four basic truths to make the people clear how these truths make the people clear, how these truths play vital role in my tantrism for its positive impact against all kinds of evil beings and harmful beings that have been a major and unavoidable problem of human life. This book though deals with abstract subject of tantrism, crosses the nearest way to reality. But it does not draw the people to confusion. As this subject is unlike the old and traditional religious actions it is quite fit to solve the mysterious and harmful activities of evil beings of the people who are suffering from diseases and who are imprisoned by evil spirits by throwing lot of unbearable, Pain and problems, follow the rules given as remedy.

THE FIRST MAJOR BASE—THE SUN

The sun is the creator of the Earth and other planets, is the creator of all life on the Earth. So the Sun is the symbol of truth, beauty and power of truth of the Earth that generates all essentials for life on the Earth to move everywhere in the universe. No life whether it is on the land or in water or in air is possible if here is no rays of the sun. All animals and inanimate beings need light or ray of the sun for their growth and existence. It is ray of the sun that provides heat and many other essences for all living beings of the Earth. Without light or ray of the sun there can't be germination of plants and trees to grow on soil. It is a wonder even for the brave world and it has been difficult though it is not impossible for great people to touch exact reality about the sun to discover how the sun shines to spread warm light for life, how the sun radiates, how long it radiates, what is the distance of the sun from the Earth and from other planets what is the circumference of the Sun and what is the weight of the Sun. Earth sees the Sun sometimes above her head and sometimes upon her head and people continuously spend lot of time to study the truth in the vast firmament. Astrologers of high vigour have studied the sun and have given the people valuable knowledge about what they have found out in the sun. Similarly the high religious persons have sprinkled deep and abstract colour of religion considering the sun as god. Scientists, geographers and many other great persons of high intellectual calibre or men of high wit have scattered their view about the Almighty Sun differently. But nobody has accurate and exact idea about the sun. This much only most of the people know that the sun is the creator of all earthly creatures. If someone

imagines of no Sun he/she must imagine it that here is no Earth no people, no any kinds of life and nothing in totality, men of letters have agreed it that the sun is the greatest to all in all sphere and nothing is fit to match with it. It can save and destroy anything of the Earth. The gravitation power of the Sun is the main strength that compels every universal organs to hang towards it. As other planets the Earth is a planet of the Sun. So the Earth is gravitised by the sun and the Earth has hung and revolved round the sun is the law of solar system. All laws of Nature that affect all things living and non living are related to solar system. So the main source of power of the Earth solely and wholly depends upon the energy of the sun. The sun is the supreme of all supremes of the Earth is the only real god of the Earth that provides all essential things for the Earth so that the motion of the Earth and living and nonlivings here could be in the smooth and natural position. In this book of mine about tantrism and its impact on human life whether it is positive or negative I have taken the sun the first and the foremost base of the tantrism have used this 'ism' to cure the mysterious and unknown diseases that could not be treated by the use of well formulated medicines. It is the sun god that sends light and heal for all livings of the Earth. Persons who deny the gift of the sun to survive life, will suffer much. It is the fact that all people are not good in the world. Only a few persons are supposed to be of great quality and minority of the total population belongs to good category. Wicked people, cruel people, merciless people and selfish people in the world have enjoyed much suppressing good and gentle people. People who are of bad and harmful nature are ranked as black, bad and abnormal beings who are taken as evil persons. Such persons always spread their evil spirits and feeling and empower over those persons who reject their selfish and bad suggestion. Evil spirits, black spirits and people of bad and black thought govern the simple and sober people by spreading their ugly activities. So all the time such spirits and people become busy in harmful activities for the human being. Such livings do not like the sun and its ray for they perform their duty and action only in dark atmosphere. So they like the night instead of the day. Such harmful spirits and people reject the gift of the sun. They live in a place where there is no ray or light of the sun. So people who live in the dark places and have no light and heat of the sun will be victim to such evil spirits and black spirits and suffer from unknown diseases. As the result, such persons show abnormality in their dealing and behaviour. Their dealing and behaviour would be a wonder for other people could not guess the dealing and behaviour and could not measure to evaluate their activities of such abnormal persons. Because of the lack of heat and light of the sun people will not be able to move the normal life smoothly and they become abnormal. Their living and feeling became differs and become the victim to evil spirits and black spirits. Such spirits always empower over them. The unnatural crying, weeping and touching of such persons would be a pain for them and problem for other persons who take care of them. The care takers of such diseased persons will be on the horns of dilemma. They could not say what to do for them and could not say anything to provide comfort for them and themselves. Due to lack of light and heat of the sun people get suffering from diseases caused by evil spirits and black spirits and rooted it deeply. Such disease could not be cured by using modern medicines but such diseases could be cured by tantrists with the help of warm pure sun light. So the sun is considered as supreme god to all man made gods and goddesses of the Earth. People worship the sun god regularly in the morning and pray with it (The sun god) to bestow upon them all happiness of life by making them free from all sorts of evil spirits and black spirits of the Earth. People who are suffering from unknown diseases and who believe that their suffering is caused by harmful and evil spirits, may be right or may not be right in their belief and thinking. But it is sure that evil and black spirits are here on the Earth and are moving every where in their own obscure style dominating time to time over human beings and ruling in the realm of humanity supplying enough suffering for the people. To get rid of suffering from such evil spirits people must take help of Sun god. It is the light and warmth of the sun god that functions as natural medicine to cure the diseases. So people who have been victim to such bad and black beings after worshipping and praying as long as they can become free. When the warmth of the sun light penetrate in the body of the sufferers or diseased persons the hidden element into the human body will go out of the body being weak. Slowly and gradually the sick persons feel well. Hope of recovery will germinate in them. Because of such wonderful power of the sun which can't be provided by other things as its alternative in this tantrism. So I have taken the sun as the first and the foremost base of my tantrism. It is the sun that made possible the life on the Earth and uncountable life of all living beings. So the sun is the life giver, the protector and promoter of all living and non-living things. The sun is every thing essential to breathe life on this soil. It is the truth, beauty, virtue and all things of the universe. The ray or light of the sun in fact is panacea which continuously offer potential thing to lengthen life of all living beings on the land, water and air. But this light is harmful for harmful spirits and black spirits of the Earth such spirits become active, strong and powerful only in gloomy and impure atmosphere of the human dwellings. In the darkness, conjested and impure atmosphere bad black and evil beings play criminal activities and create lot of pain and problems in the body of good, simple and gentle creatures. So at night those evil spirits and other kinds of black spirits enter in human dwellings. They play dirty merciless game to quench their sinful thirst. Such spirits enjoy lot when people shed tears in pain, when people roam here and there being in loss of sense, when people cry and walk on the road being mad and when people run to grave and tomb. Men of virtue like hermits, monks etc. using various religious codes were and are busy in getting people rid of such cruel activities of evil and black beings. But all religious codes or remedies have different colours. One's method is different from other's. They also have taken to use ray or light of the sun as a major element in treatment. They also advise the people to worship the sun god to gain queer strength so that the sufferers from evil and black spirits could be strong enough mentally and physically on the one hand and could be victor instead of being victim of such harmful beings on the other. Their concept is certainly fine and critical though they have founded many imaginary idol of gods and goddesses of power to be free from fear and tear for themselves and to make other people the same.

In this book of mine I have included four major bases of power to make tantric colour effective and permanent in human life. The sun is the first great base of power of this book which has been quite different in quality than other three bases.

The sun is shadow casting base but other three bases have other three different qualities. The sun's ray is the combination of seven colour known as 'spectrum' So in my tantrism I have taken the sun as body of the 'ism'. The main functions of the sun in this subject are *(a)* To maintain the human body healthy. *(b)* To remove all kinds of weakness of human beings by providing heat *(c)* Provide moral integrity and *(d)* Smooth motion of human life. Again ray of the sun is such powerful element all evil spirits can't appear to fall upon any persons on the narrow ground of selfish motive to take revenge upon them or to quench thirst of human blood. It is all accepted and believed fact that in Nepal here are many gods and goddesses of various power in religions. People here worship and pray Lords for happiness and all other good things. But they do not know whether their wishes and desires could be fulfilled or not by those supreme Lords of power. All those supreme Lords of the people are Earthly Lords with limited sphere on the Earth. Sometimes some people used to think that it is hollow belief of the people that gods and goddesses can do any thing for the people. They think if Lords are pleased they will bless them abundant happiness and if Lords are angry they will curse them and get miseries. As the result of god's cursing people fall into bad to worst condition for long time. So it is advised the people not to be blind followers and no to be dependant all the time upon the mercy of gods and goddesses but to be reasonable by developing the habit of believing in human strength and real strength of the sun.

My this book intends to draw people's attention to reality and reason by throwing their blind belief and superstition away from the mind. It also this book intends to pour more potential knowledge of religion and tantrism to make people more gain by putting them away from voidness. As the Sun is the main base or body of my tantrism I advise people to get up with the sun, move every where with the sun and sleep soundly with the sun. Such habit will, if adopted by people, be quite useful and fruitful to lead the life on the Earth without falling on the horns of dilemma. People of thought who venture to get success in life must leave all grumbling because of uneasy and risky complication. They should not be in the habit of confusion, fear depending upon other. They should lead life plainly. Simple and straight forward life of the people is the best life. So believe in the sun and its measureless strength. Human life must be pure and sure as the Sun. The Sun is Sun. Nothing can be compared with the Sun because of such unsurpassable power of the Sun. I have placed the sun the basic major power of my tantrism. If the people have to hide belief in their mind hide this belief. There is the Sun above and upon their head for ever and shines for ever as only one real Almighty of the Earth.

THE SECOND MAJOR BASE—AIR

The second major base of the tantrism that I have brought in light to make people know about its importance in human life, is Air. Air is a wonderful and powerful natural element as essential and as pure as the sun light. But the characteristic of air is different from the sun's *(a)* Air is invisible *(b)* It is colourless *(c)* Air is light and movable it can blow vastly *(d)* It is the product of nature *(e)* invisibility is its another quality *(f)* Mixture of gases *(g)* Measureless and limitless. Air is life without air no living beings whether they are men or animals or plants or insects or birds exist on the Earth. In this tantrism I have taken air as second major base to use as breathing of tantrism. Body without respiration is death. As the sun is placed as body air is used as respiration of this tantrism with the help of air life moves every where. Free blowing of pure air is the most essential thing to get rid of all unhealthy atmospheric things to be away from catching by bad, black and evil spirits. Black spirits and evil spirits like witches, wizards, fantoms, ghosts and many other kinds of harmful livings can't prevail any handicaps such as pain and problems over ordinary or normal human beings unless they live in dark and unventilated place. Pure smooth and normal blowing of air helps to check evil elements and other harmful black elements. So such elements can't reach in human dwellings. But in case of abnormal blowing of air it may give change to harmful spirits and evil spirits to raise up their head to pull persons of simple and gentle temperament to the risk by adding more complications in their life. When air does not blow in normal state it will be abnormal in blowings. The blowing of air in more high speed or in very low speed is considered as abnormal blowing of air. The high blowing or low blowing of air both are considered as abnormality of air in blowing. It is good and favourable chance for bad and evil spirits to enter in residence of human beings if air blows in abnormal speed. The religion has proved it that persons of high virtue as well as high vice both holding tantric practices for required period fly far and wide to long distance with the help of blowing air. Such persons can reach to their destination flying in the air. People who are expert in tantric practice can easily fly to different parts of the country and sometimes they fly from one country to other countries too. It is known as spiritual flight. So air is very important factor in religion to show the tantric strength and it is equally important in science. In the scientific movement also air has played vital role to demonstrate its wonderful strength to the people of the world. Persons who apply tantric procedures for healing pain and problems of the people take help of air. The evil spirits and black spirits also on the other hand with the help of air move to different places to

fall upon the body of persons with a view to create ugly harmful effect on them. There will be unexpected bad effect in human life when evil beings enter in human life when evil beings and harmful being flow with air and enter in human body secretly. Disturbance caused by evil spirit is wonderful, painful and unbearable for the people. When black spirits hide secretly in human body they move secretly in human body they move time to time from one to another part of the body and create very hard pain in the person's life. It is the fact that persons with the help of air can do various flights in the world. Spiritual flight, physical flight and material flight are three kinds of main flights people enjoy in their life. But such flights are possible only when there is enough air blowing on the Earth. But in this book I have illustrated only about spiritual flight. Good spirits and bad spirits both make flight with air in the world good spirits are good and thing of joy for living beings. But bad and black spirits make flight in air with wicked intention. They visit far and wide in human dwellings to spread miseries in life. So air though it is invisible immeasurable, indivisible etc. has unsurpassable strength is used for good luck and bad luck of the people.

I have taken air as second major base of the tantrism to use it as a high power natural element to be used to fight with evil spirits and black spirits so that any bad and harmful spirits could not venture in the dwellings of human beings to pour pain and problem for any person. Blowing pure air of the morning from dawn to 7 o'clock is taken to use for the tantric purpose. So those persons who are in trouble and getting pain and problems from evil spirits and black spirits should go at the top deck of the house or should go out from the house to open ground. They should take seven round of human body length on the ground. If they go at the top of the deck of the house they should take twenty one to forty nine round of the human body length everyday without missing even a single day. After taking round they should have sun bath for seven minutes or more. This is the medical side of the tantrism. In fact nothing is artificial in the long run all things are produced with the help of nature and are used as free gift of Nature changing only shape and size of the things. Air is one of the free gift of Nature. It must be accepted by all living beings and must be used properly, and carefully to enjoy the real fun of it in life. But in this tantrism simple air and the spelled air both are used for the treatment. Simple air is purely natural air where as the spelled air is tantric air. When some secret spell is poured in the simple air it is spelled air. Simple air is for all living beings to move life. But simple air sometimes may be impure in quality because of the mixture of various polluted factors as smoke particle of dust and dirt. Time to time evil spirits and harmful black spirits also reach in human dwelling invisibly mixing in air. So people must be quite beware of such evil beings and must be careful of such spheric danger. Air in the congested place is impure air. Such congested place is the most favourable place for such harmful spirits. They arrive in such places and attack upon persons. So open space is place to lead life in peace. But in this tantrism air is used as second major base of it has solid validity to be used as an effective remedy to cure unknown diseases caused by evil spirits. So here is concerned more about the spelled air. When such tantric spelled air is used for the patients they can be fit to walk their life in a normal way. The hidden effect of the evil spirits in the human body will be weak in the continuous use of the spelled air for certain required period. At last such spirits can't resist the power of the spelled air and escape from human body. Then diseased persons will be free from evil catching. Through air evil spirits enter in human body to enjoy for themselves by creating pain and problems and move away from the body of the patient being unable to digest the spelled air. So it is suggested not to live in congested and dark place. Air of such place is impure air where evil spirits dance there being happy to their success in creating problems for all simple and gentle people.

THE THIRD MAJOR BASE—WATER

Among the four major bases of my tantrism I have placed water in third rank. This liquid material also is the queer gift of Nature which is helpful for all living beings to be fit to live on the Earth. Water is such important colourless pure things in liquid form is as essential as other bases sun light and air. But unlike sun light and air water is liquid, touchable, visible and drinkable thing though it can't be measured in simple way. Both movable and immovable life need water to live on the Earth. It is water which is considered as holy thing of the Earth. So people of different religions regard it as mother or father. Hindu regards the flowing river Ganga as Mata other regard it as Father Nile. Men whoever and wherever they may be need water to quench their thirst and for many purposes. Irrigation of land for farming, is impossible without water. For hydro power water is equally important for men. So men seek water. In fact existence of life on the Earth is quite impossible if here is no water. So Hindus worship the river considering it as goddess. What is water when and how water flow on the Earth is difficult to know exactly. This much only people know about water is it is nature made thing gifted to all living beings to lead life happily on the Earth whether they are living on the soil, or in water or in air. Water is life. It is used in every field of human activities. Religion has used water in its all religious activities science also uses it to turn to success miraculously.

But in this tantrism I have taken water to use it as *(a)* Holy liquid medicine *(b)* liquid thing to push away evil spirits and all types of harmful black spirits from human body *(c)* A thing of continuity of procedure in tantrism *(d)* A thing to purify other materials used an ingredients of tantrism and *(e)* A thing to diagnose the unknown disease and its nature caused by harmful evil spirits. It is water that filters nature of human beings to put away unnatural lingerings in life. When evil spirits and black spirits dominate normal nature of the persons water will be used to weaken the dominating evil power. Simple water is natural one which is used to purify the outward things required for the tantric performance. Taking bath washing hands and feet of the patients is done through simple water. But for

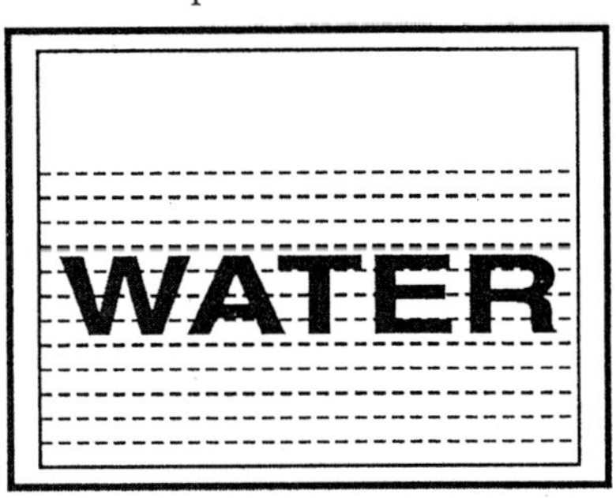

inward complications of the body and vivid symptoms of unknown disease caused by evil spirits and black spirits in persons the spelled water is prepared to be used as medicine. Such spelled water is powerful water used to cure the diseases. The water should be used by the patients as directed them by the healer for days. The day can be extended to use the spelled water up to forty nine days as the maximum days to use the spelled water as medicine for the diseases. As water is taken the third major base of the tantrism it can be used in all sectors of tantrism. This water should be offered to the guard pot, to the Mandala and to the black thread used in the guard pot and Mandala before its use to the patient if there is installed guard pot and Mandala at home. Another thing about the use of water is to maintain peace and harmonious atmosphere in the dwellings. Sometimes black spirits and many kinds of evil spirits appear in human dwelling. They disturb human beings. In the dwellings those evil creatures create horror, quarrelling among persons, discontent, sudden shouting, crying, weeping, unexpected fear and surprise etc. The solution for all such problems and complications in the human dwellings is water-the spelled water. The spelled water is the only solution for any harmful works and actions of such spirits. In the human dwellings when there appear evil spirits like ghosts, shadowy fantoms, Skeltonic figures etc. and spread fear and horror time to time the spelled water should be sprinkled all over the dwellings in guided time and in guided way. It is certain that such sprinkling of the spelled water in the human dwellings will weakness the ruling of the evil spirits and all kinds of harmful black spirits and they will be nowhere within a few days. Perhaps people will be in doubt about the preparation method of the spelled or magic like powerful water to be used as a tantric water to weaken and to put away evil spirits at last for ever. So I want to make people sure how to prepare the spelled water. Take a cup of simple and pure water and write the seven symbolic tantric letters as shown in Mandala with the help of the scissors use only one blade of the scissors to write the symbolic letters in the water. Again write the name of the patient or the persons to whom it is made to use. All the words as witches, wizards, ghosts, skeltonic fantoms etc. also should be written in the water. Give short breath seven times in the water. Smoke of insane also should be given to the water to convert it as spelled one. Then mix it to simple water. The simple water should be enough for 7 days to drink for the patient. Every time in the morning at 7 o'clock and at night also at 7 the concerned person should drink seven tea spoon the spelled water regularly. If the effect of the spelled water is good continue it for other 7 days. This is the way to prepare the spelled water. The dose for the patient to drink the spelled medicine holy water is once a day for light or normal case and twice a day for hard or old case. But every time seven teaspoon should be drunk. In the use of such spelled or magic like holy water to get rid of evil spirits persons who use it should be very careful and must follow these conditions *(a)* the spelled water should not be put on floor or on the ground *(b)* It should be used for the concerned person only not for other person. If is made for a particular house to sprinkle, it should not be used in other house. *(c)* Seven teaspoonful spelled water should be drunk in a time. If it is made for the house seven palmful spelled water should be sprinkle in the house. But these seven palmful water should cover every nook and corner of the house. *(d)* This spelled water should not be used for a child not older than seven months *(e)* It should not be for lunatics and disabled persons by birth *(f)* The spelled water pot should be kept out of children's reach *(g)* Don't add other simple water in it and don't put it in refrigerator. *(h)* Put the spelled water pot in secret place so that it could not be seen by other persons *(i)* Put the pot in the same place where you put it first. *(j)* The spelled water pot should have seven round black thread on its neck. *(k)* The lid of the pot should be closed tightly so that no bad air of evil spirits and black spirits could enter in it. All these given conditions should be followed strictly. This spelled water can be prepared by any body who have great interest in this field if they are taught the method once. My tantrism is open secret for all on the one hand and liberal construction on the other. Persons whoever they may be can learn all techniques and procedures for their safety as well as for the safety of their relatives, friends and good wishes. But those who have no belief or no interest in such subject can't enjoy any sweet fruit of this abstract subject. Again people of coward or weak nature also can't enjoy any fruit of this subject. Any steam whether it is the spelled air or the spelled water will be useful for nothing for them. So do not use the spelled water for such weak persons.

THE FOURTH MAJOR BASE—LAND

The fourth major base of this tantrism is land. This is the last base of the tantrism. All living beings whoever and whichever they may be can't live in the air for ever though they can roam or fly in the air for some period. Common human can live above the land for certain hours or days with the help of aeroplane of spacecraft. But they all must drop or came back to land. Land is the most essential pre requisite for all living beings. Those living beings are persons, animals, birds, insects, plant and trees. Land means the surface of the Earth. Some surface of the Earth are solid, some are watery and some are dry. On all surfaces there are life. I have taken here to include in this book is only the land where human beings are dwelling. The weight of human beings on the land known as density. The human beings whether they are normal or abnormal have been heavier and heavier in every passes of year. At present hundreds of billions of people are the inhabitants of the Earth. Many inhabitants are good and normal and some are bad and wicked ones. People are suffering much from such wicked and evil people. Witches and wizards are evil persons are being pain and problem for the people dwelling peacefully on the land. Various extra ordinary bad and black spirits also are recently moving on the land everywhere scattering various kinds of trouble in human life ghost, fantoms, skeltonic living and gonams etc. belong to such category. They also some way or other live and move on the land. This book intends to help people of common and simple nature in tantric way to make them live and move on the land easily to lead life happily being free from all kinds of evil spirits. Land allocated for human dwelling should be protected from the attack of harmful evil beings. It is not easy task to erect bar

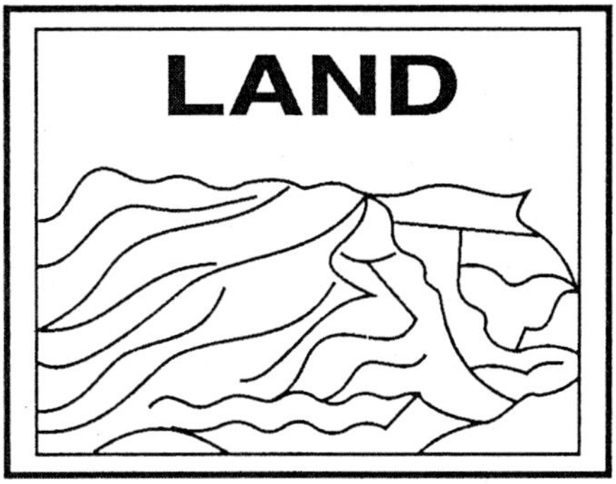

to check such spirits to enter in human dwelling because most of the movement of such spirits are invisible. They, all of sudden, appear in the house for people's horror fear and tear in the life of the people. The existence of such spirits have been topic of the people to solve the ugly problem. But there has not been still hard and fast rules or codes to eliminate them completely. In the old religion there are may various tantric strength based on purely religious ritual spell to put an end to such harmful spirits. Various religious persons have made some religious things using ritual spell to use as remedy to be free from bad, black and harmful spirits as well as evil spirits which are known as jantra. Jantras can be found in different strength or capacity as relief to be safe or free from the attack of evil and black spirits. Such jantras help people to protect them and also their residential land not to be influenced by those harmful beings. Land of the Earth is common plane to all good and bad, useful and harmful living beings. Sometimes the land is used by uncommon livings too. These uncommon or extra ordinary livings are evil beings or angles. They time to time arrive on the land of human beings and apply their power and demonstrate their strength for and against will of simple ordinary and common persons. People's duty is to greet good spirits like angels and hate evil spirits like devils, fantoms, gonams etc. In the land of the people bad harmful beings should not be permitted to take motion according to their will by devouring human life. So land should be protected. Lot of labour is being done in this field. But in this tantrism land is counted as fourth major base and it has special role to play to free the people from evil beings and black beings by checking them to enter in human dwellings. The human land should be protected land that is quite free and fearless land. No destructive and harmful evil and black spirits in any conditions could venture to step in human doors to harm any innocent, simple and normal beings. To maintain such safety in the human land this tantrism with certain conditions or limitations should be applied. The limitations or conditions are *(a)* Human dwellings specially the home should be neat and clean, open and ventilated *(b)* There must be sunlight in day time and electric or oil light at night in the house there should not be dark at all, *(c)* specially the black cat and mole should not be allowed to enter to move here and there in the house *(d)* Fantastic and super natural topics should not be entered to talk in the house by the members of the house. *(e)* Woman of matured age should not be suppressed and threatened unnecessarily to make them loose their normal nature. *(f)* Children of below seven years should not be sent out of the house after evening and at night. *(g)* Mandala with guard pot should be installed in the house. The fourth major base the land has its own peculiarities as other three major bases have. What to talk of religion and science every thing also have their own special and particular base on the land in equal strength and capacity. It is the true concept of the people that no religion can flourish in any part of the world without its deep root in the land of human dwellings. Similar is the importance of the land in the field of science. On the Earth there is no possibility of existence of the both science and religion which are considered as body and soul of humanity. Men of thoughts and men of action both had lived on the land since the time immemorial and still living on the earth without any breach following all rules or laws of Nature. No creation is possible without the land on the Earth. So in this tantrism land is considered and taken as fourth major base.

In the tantrism the first base is visible, untouchable, indivisible, immeasurable and warm element. The second one is invisible untouchable indivisible immeasurable and cold element. It is a kind of gas. The third base is visible, touchable indivisible immeasurable and cold element. It is a liquid element. The fourth base is divisible artificially, visible, touchable, measurable and mild warm element. It is a solid element. All these four major bases of this tantrism have their different and similar qualities. Two are touchable and two are not touchable. Three are visible and one is invisible. One is red hot solid and out of human reach and one is gray mild hot and human can reach in any part of it. Two are solid. One is liquid and one is gas. These four major bases which are entirely different in shape and size, colour and kind, quality and taste, volume and compactness etc. are pure and Natural products. They are real divine powers of this tantrism that bring certain solid achievements in human life. They are the symbol of truth and beauty that can easily general harmony among the people to lead real fearless life. No livings or elements of the Earth whether they are for good or for bad can match these four major bases of this tantrism are matchless without any possibility of alternatives. So this tantrism is not the product of fabrication, illusion, superstition imitation supposition etc. rather it is powerful production of spontaneous flow of unique power of the combination of four major bases the sun, the air, the water and the land.

So unlike other going on tantrisms of Nepal it has lot of new things which are quite effective and can be applied easily by any persons who have faith in it. Those who with faith if apply rules and regulations of this tantrism, I am sure they can taste wonderfully healthy things in life and will be happy soul without facing any kinds of obstacles on the way to forwarding.

THE INTER RELATION OF TANTRISM WITH OTHER SUBJECTS

Tantrism has been closely inter related with other subjects. It has inseparable relation with religion and close relation with other social sciences. It's relationship with morality and human physiology and psychology is vast and deep. But in this chapter I have to narrate the relation of tantrism with religion and science first because these topics are important subjects and have subtle and adverse impact upon it to do good sometimes and bad another time.

Religion and tantrism

Religion and tantrism are twin subjects. One is soul and another is body. In absence of one another does not function effectively. Every religion has its tantric side to take its complete form. It will be no wrong to say that religion is theological theory and tantrism is its practice. In other words, religion is beautiful flower bloomed in pure ethical orchard and tantrism is its scent. All religions whether it is Hinduism or Buddhism or any other religion of the world they have their practical side that is known as tantrism. In Hindu religion there are many laws or codes which are quite effective when they are put in practice. The spiritual flights if done following laws of religion, can be done to reach to quite distance to visit to designated human dwellings or to visit to abodes of gods and goddesses. It can be done to enter in human body without making know to other people. All supreme beings gods and goddesses according to Hindu religion can easily fly from one place to any other places according to their need to fulfil their desire whether it is good or bad for other. Such flying of persons or of supreme beings is certainly the practical beauty of the religion is counted as tantric strength of the religion. The sudden appearance of angels in human dwellings is benevolent side of tantric action but the appearance of evil spirits and black spirits is bad and harmful side of tantrism. These both sides are available in Hindu religion. The Sadhus, sages, monks etc. of Hindu religion have high power of spiritual flight using such unique power. They reach in any places of their need. Sometimes they disguising themselves as different creatures visit to different places. They fly in various ways time to time to surprise people, to help the people and to punish or reward the people is certainly the tantric quality of religion.

A sudden visit of Lord Krishna, Lord Shiva, Lord Bishnu etc. goddess Parbati goddess Durga, goddess Radha etc. disguising themselves as ordinary beings as terrible beings, as helpful beings reach time to time here and there to create wonder and surprise are certainly the tantric events of Hindu religion. Such wonderful and surprising events of Lords and goddesses on the one hand and fearful horrible and painful events of the evil spirits and black spirits of the religion on the other are two antagonistic sides of the religion. Similar events of wonder and surprise are available in Buddhism too. In Buddhism too Buddhist monks and sages holding high meditation can fly spiritually to far distance. It is heard they also can fly from one part of the country to other and from one country to another. They also can fly with a view to settle in human body. They also can create various kinds of miracles to make the people wonder or surprise. Is it not the tantric side of this religion? Certainly yes. So it can be said undoubted that religion and tantrism are two inseparable things that move hand in hand every moment in every place of human dwellings creating various impacts in the life of the people. The healers always take good quality of tantrism to make the sufferers happy so sages, monks hermits who serve the sufferers from evil spirits, and black and bad spirits have possessed good tantric power to heal them whereas wicked and narrow minded selfish persons have gained only bad power of tantrism such persons being witches and wizards create pain and problems in human life to take revenge upon those who are not liked by them, who had behaved them impolitely, who had not fulfilled the things that they had asked for with them. It is said that there is tantrism where there is religion and there is religion where there is tantrism people who adept the religion which ever it may be Hinduism, Buddhism or any other religion can't take religion only putting its other side the tantrism. As religion is an abstract subject its tantric side also is abstract though its result is concrete one. So most of the people when they fall in tantric sphere of the religion can't believe it and its effect on human life because such effect is mostly subjective in colour. But people believe in tantric impact when they get its impact on their own life. As religion is performed in individual style and desire tantric performance also is done in the same style and fulfil their desire. Persons who have been victim to the evil spirits and all kinds of black spirits believe in the existence of such spirits in many parts of human dwellings. Persons who have suffered much from such bad, black and harmful spirits, visit to healers. So it is not difficult to see the people rushing to the sages, monks and hermits' house for tantric healing. I have read in books that the Buddhist monks of Shri Lanka, Burma, Thailand have possessed very high tantric power and used it for the human service to make the people free from suffering from evil spirits and black spirits. Similar study I have done in Hindu religion too and knew how the hermits, sages and monks made spiritual flight and how they healed the people suffering from bad and black spirits. Almighty gods and goddesses are described in other religion besides Hinduism and Buddhism. Good beings as well as bad beings are found to be described in other religions. From all events occurrences, appearances of all kinds of super and supreme beings described in various religions it has been clear that because of various reasons of different religions such good and evil spirits are originated and made enough ground to play in human residential areas sometimes positively and another time negatively. The tantric role of the religion has shown the vivid pictures by giving motion of the super and supreme beings both good and bad, beneficial and harmful, simple and complicated motion, to turn the luck of the ordinary and common persons. But such close, interwoven virtue of religion and tantrism became dim and dark because of mishandling and misinterpretation by the concerned persons in the passage of time. At present the position of these subjects has been false and people began to laugh at. It is considered as baseless and dreamy topics. But whatever is the version of the people it is the fact that there are still religion and tantrism in motion to influence the people. Both are closely linked each other in Nepal. Still it is quite applicable in day to day life of the Nepalese people and more percent of people of Nepal are still following the doctrines and principles of religion and tantrism to pass their life in normal and simple style.

Science and tantrism

Though science and tantrism are entirely different subjects and quite antagonistic in nature they are similar in their action and practical used in many ways. Tantrism is the practical side of religion. Many rules are there in the religion that can be applied in day to day life of the people positively some times and negatively another time. The positive effect is caused by the good spirits as angles and other heavenly living beings where as the negative effect is caused by evil spirits and harmful bad and black spirits. Monks, sages, hermits etc. use religious codes or power positively to snow the tantric effect as miracles to heal the suffering. They used most of the beneficial religious law to provide happiness in human life. But evil and black spirits such as witches, wizards, fantoms, ghost skeltonic beings gonams etc. use religious rules to fall human beings in pain and problems. So such action of evil spirits is not good rather creates negative impact on human beings. Tantrism is as old as religion and older then science. Tantric activity is spiritual that's why it is difficult to measure and to present or display its visual picture to bring it to clear understanding for ordinary people. Most of the tantric actions are abstract and mysterious on the one hand and differ according to personal differentiation on the other. It has no accurate value and weight, no shape and size, no material validity etc. except moral and ethical significance. The strength of tantrism is counted in term of its peculiar action to produce more effect in human life. Tantrism has many secret ritual spells and are systematic codes of actions to touch the goal. All religious codes of tantrism are brought in use to solve all kinds of simple as well as mysterious pains and problems of the people are the valid and vivid events of Nepal since the ancient time. In Nepal since the time immemorial people have been in great use of tantrism as their requirement for their happiness. In those by gone days, centpercent people of Nepal would believe in tantrism as it had high power in many human activities. Tantrism belongs to religious science but it has close relation with natural science. In fact science is a collection of systematic laws which are effective every time for every person. Law of gravity, laws of tide, law of number and many other laws are all laws of pure science. Science is bounded power which produces many types of good and harmful things for the people. If science is applied properly and carefully certainly it is good for the people to move ahead for the betterment of humanity. But it is up to human desire about how to use the science. People can use science for good or for bad. If it is used for good people will sleep with peace and rise with peace. If they use science for bad purpose they will shed tears in repentance and pass the night without sleep. This modern age is highly influenced by science. In major walk of life science has played vital role. It has been successful to cater many useful comfortable and wonderful things all over the world that have been great help for the people to pass life in ease. People know it very well that every thing has bright good and useful impact on human beings at the same time it has harmful, bad risky and poisonous effect too. Science also has both qualities good and bad. It is good for human beings because it has invented many useful, beautiful and wonderful things has helped to make pace of life fast, long and easy. Certainly this is the optimistic side of the science. But science to break peace into piece of human mind and human strength of oneness, has created lot of destructive means of ugly use as gun, rocket, missiles, atom bomb etc. which dash people to go to dog. Such creations have disturbed the world to be unsafe place for all living beings. So pros side of the science must be increased by reducing cons side of it for sweet upliftment of the world. Science and tantrism both are the subjects for human beings. Some people take science because they have faith in it some people favour tantrism because they have faith in it. So what is great thing is human faith. Faith is great thing in every aspect of human life. Because of faith some embrace science and some the tantrism what science can't do can be done by tantrism and what tantrism can't do can be done by science. So both these subjects are equally powerful. One is not superior or inferior to other. Both are useful for the people if they know how to use them for their benefit. People must use both science and tantrism very carefully, faithfully and honestly according to their need. People should not be one sided rather should be multi sided to measure the value of things whether they belong to science or to tantrism. Critical in thinking and keen in observation help people to gain more fruits from science or from the tantrism. In fact tantrism is also science. But it is socio-religious science that deals with human beings' behaviour and nature. It is originated for the human welfare that provides abundant benefit for lasting life.

So science and tantrism must move hand in hand to make the people fearless and happy. The people must be able to balance both science and tantrism to pass the life in normal state with maximum enjoyment that are hanging around them as sweet of tantrism and science.

Tantrism and psychology

Tantrism is religious activity that influences upon human life sometimes directly and sometimes indirectly by creating benefit and harm to turn human life to different destinations. It can't be pushed away by the people till the end of life. Psychology is the subject that deals with contents of mind of the people. It is the science which helps the people to find out the hidden things in the mind of the people by observing the face, by looking into behaviours, by listening the way of talking and style of the movement. It is psychology that measures human beings position by studying their mind's construction in their face. If a man is quite innocent, if a man is strong or frail physically or mentally, if a man is simple or complex or suffering from certain pain and problems or enjoying in life or in quite happy can be known through psychological study. All kinds of human symptoms also can be found with the help of psychological study. Tantrism also is directly related to human luck. One who is happy can be turned to miserable state if people become victim to evil spirits and harmful black spirits. If one who is in trouble, pain and problems can be turned into happy person if good spirits favour him/her. It is all sweet and sour fruit of tantrism. Tantric healing will be successful if the healers know the psychological set up of the patients. So in many fields of tantric healing and dealings psychological impact is valued and is considered greatly because of close link between these two subjects. In human life psychology has functioned silently and vastly but effectively to change mood of the people. But tantrism functioned silently and vastly but effectively to change mood of the people. But tantrism functions as sudden waves that creates different quakes in all parts of the body of the people. So tantric healers who can touch the hidden feeling of the people can get easy way to heal the people when they fall in uneasy condition due to fabrication of evil spirits. So it is sure that tantrism and psychology are closely related each other.

Tantrism and history

It is well known fact to all people that every subject has it own history to tell the past events of the concerned subject. Tantrism has also its own history. It tells people how it had influenced the people by occurring wonderful and thundered miracles upon the life of the people to turn their destiny from brightness to gloominess, from happiness to misery and from solid state to liquid state. What was the strength of tantric activity in the past how did the people suffer from evil and harmful black spirits, what was the role of the tantrism in those bygone days all these things can be known with help of history of tantrism. So people who have great interest to know all past events of tantrism and its performance to control the evil and black living beings they must turn the pages of the history eagerly to find about reality of this subject. It is said that tantrism is as old as religion. It had spread its wings to fly everywhere in humanity scatterings wonder to amaze the people when science was just in the womb.

As the perimeter or say the scope of the tantrism is deep rooted in soil of humanity and as old as religion it has link with other subjects too as mathematic, philosophy, Economics, Ethic etc. in some way or other. So while studying or practising tantrism persons must think to know how mathematic philosophy, Economics, Ethic etc. in some way or other. So while studying or practising tantrism persons must think to know how mathematic philosophy, Ethic etc. have chested their colour in it.

MEDITATION

Meditation is only one way to salvation. Though it is easy to say very hard to move on with it to the destination. Persons who try to walk spiritually through meditation they have to face many kinds of complications as obstacles that always dash the meditators to move back instead of forwarding in motion. One thing that I want to clear here is the tantric meditation is more difficult than simple meditation. Major complications that appear in the tantric meditation are *(a)* greediness *(b)* Anger *(c)* Ignorance *(d)* Proudness *(e)* Selfishness *(f)* Extreme passion *(g)* Excessive hope and desire *(h)* Depression. These all mentioned complications are major obstacles on the way to salvation through tantric meditation. Persons who venture to hold meditation for salvation must be in firm determination as hard as iron to be successful in the regular course. All those lingering weaknesses of the people that are mentioned above from (A) to (H) must be buried somewhere away taking out from the mind. If there remains any one of the mentioned complications in the person it will destroy the required strength and can't be successful to reach to destination.

If anybody want to hold the tantric meditation as shown in the attached picture herewith they must prepare that tantric Mandap for meditation and must start it being in given directions. This kind of meditation provides unique different taste which is superior to ordinary meditation. It is this meditation which provided high inspiration to different fields of life. That's why it is better to practise this meditation to be rich in spiritual happiness in life. Another thing that should be known is patience is compulsory for those who want to learn this tantrism. One who sincerely starts the tantric meditation he/she will gain a perennial source of happiness in the long run though it has been a bit difficult in the beginning. There may appear above mentioned weakness or obstacles or complications on the way and force him/her to abandon it. But persons of firm determination who have capacity to overcome all complications enjoy a lot by holding such tantric meditation. This kind of tantric meditations has many benefits but no harms at all. This kind of meditation helps to obtain enjoyment which is super one and helpful to taste peculiar happiness in life unknown to ordinary meditators. The soul of the meditator of this tantric meditation will be filled with truth, disciplinary beauty, fearlessness, physical and mental controlling power, spiritual flight, flow of potentiality for sound health, sacrifice etc. Gain of such meditation is abstract in quality but useful in application to broaden the mind. Now I write a few lines to make people clear about how to start this tantric meditation. First look the mediation Mandap. Some know how can be found out from the Mandap sketch the mandap as shown in the picture on the ground or in a thick paper should be made. Sit in the middle of the sketched Mandap. Starting should be done through East direction on Saturday. In each direction the meditation should be of seven days (From Saturday to Friday) For next week the direction should be changed from East to South. In this direction meditation should be done for seven days (From Saturday to Friday). Change the direction from South to West and continue meditation for seven days (from Saturday to Friday) then again change the direction from West to North direction. In this North direction also seven days must be used for meditation from Saturday to Friday. This cyclical method should be repeated without any break for months and years. More the meditation people hold more the people gain from it and they will be successful to reach to salvation scattering lot of truth, disciplinary beauty, fearlessness, control of power, spiritual flight, flow of potentiality, sacrifice, soundness in health etc. More the people bend to salvation less will be the complications on the way. At last they will not get any complications far meditation. In this stage the meditators will be a great meditators. They can fly any where spiritually according to their need. Again one thing more about the meditation in tantric method is the suitable time and duration of meditation Time is 7 o'clock in the morning. The duration of time is twenty one minutes in the beginning. It could be extended up to forty nine minutes as maximum time duration for the tantric meditation. Meditation should be moved on and on from east to south, South to west and west to North directions. In this way meditation should be done without any break and obstruction. Eyes should be completely closed, mind should be void. Here void means there should not be any hope, fear, greediness, proudness etc. in the mind of the persons who are going to meditate. They must pull more possible faces, places events as close as possible to the eyes. They must pull many possible places of historical importance before their eyes. In time of pulling things, places and persons, face through meditation if by chance unknown or never seen things, places or persons appear before the eyes they should know them by doing silent inquiry to themselves. If people could not know things, places and persons they should cast away from their memory or mind there and then the pulling and pushing things, places and persons according to the need can be done in meditation. But in case of tantric meditation the pulling and pushing game through meditation is different from ordinary meditation. In ordinary meditations the meditators used to pull and push ordinary things places and persons But in this tantric meditation places to be pulled before the eyes are temples, graves, inns, monasteries, things, to be pulled before the eyes are all required things to perform tantric performances and persons to be pulled are witches wizards, ghosts and many other evil spirits and black spirits. According to the need even healers also are pulled before the eyes. This is the pulling exercise of meditators.

As to pushing the meditators must push away all those harmful things that hamper the body and that disturbs the meditation. Harmful drinking such as wine, beer and other alcoholic drinks and smoking also should be given up. Such things should be pushed away by the meditators from their memory. Places that cause mental disturbances such as prostitution, theft centres linking places fighting and killing places should be taken away from the memory. Such harmful places should be pushed away soon to get success in meditation. Harmful evil spirits black spirits wicked persons should be pushed away so that they could not do any evil work for the persons to meditate.

Pull and push are two very essential antagonistic poles. Between these two poles the meditation functions to gain spiritual purity and beauty to lead human life successful and to move ahead to salvation. Through tantric meditation people must pull good persons, super beings, supreme beings etc. at the same time evil beings, black harmful beings all disturbing elements should be pushed away to make them out of sight and out of mind for ever. It is meditation that helps people to be free from all sorts of lacking by filling mind and memory with spiritual calibre or strength that works as fuel to run the life smoothly on the Earth. But tantric meditation is unique light in which all kinds of evil beings harmful beings, bad and black beings die.

Now I want to assure the people who want to take this tantric meditation that it helps the people to pass life in a simple and easy way being free all the time from the pain and problems created by evil spirits and all kinds of harmful black spirits. This meditation is not to fly to far distance where human can't reach. It is only for finding out how harmful spirits for human beings move in and out in human dwellings, how to be free from their ugly and merciless attack, how to control those spirits and how to get easy relief from all kinds of diseases caused by witches, wizards, ghosts, fantoms etc.

My this tantric meditation unlike other religious and other different kinds of meditations is suitable for those persons who are regularly suffering from evil beings to be safe from such beings and to be able to put them out of sight and out of mind. People of Nepal, as they are highly dominated by the blind superstition always think about evil spirits, black spirits and imaginary fantoms and feel suffering from such things. Too much is harmful for the people. People of Nepal are in trouble due to too much belief in nothing. They have lot of superstitious belief that's why they are suffering much due to their blind faith. If they minimise such blind faith by themselves being active to push away their such weakness certainly they will not suffer much from bad harmful elements. The best method of curing caused by evil and harmful elements is in the hand of sufferers themselves. They must be quite strong mentally and throw all blind faith taking out form their mind.

My this tantric meditation is quite helpful and useful for those people who are in high blind faith. So it is my advice to hold this tantric meditation to follow all the things shown in the meditation Mandap strictly. All the conditions also should be followed by the meditators of this meditation to get unexpected benefit form it. At length, I express the best wishes for all people who are ready to take this meditation for their happy life. Let not fall any evil beings and black harmful beings shadow on and in human body is my good wishes.

MEDITATION MANDAP

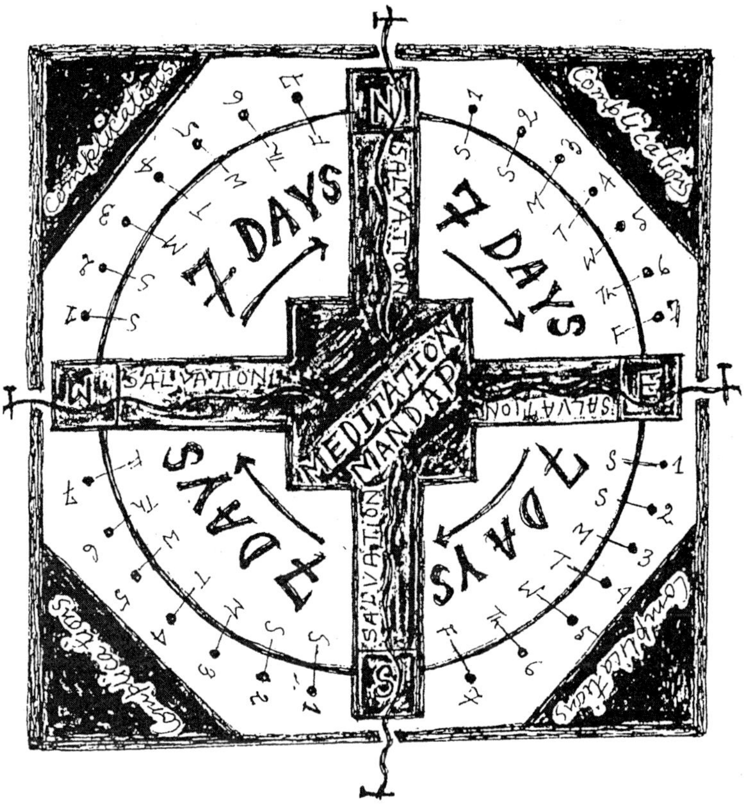

- Starting from East to South, South to West, West to North Repeat it in clock-wise way.
- Seven days meditation for one direction
- The black nail knotted thread should be but in the sitting place for meditation
- Knotted side should be kept out straight to the direction.
- Time duration for meditation is 21 minutes for beginner. It should be increased up to 49 minutes
- Starting day is Saturday.
- Complications : *(a)* Greediness
  (b) Anger

(*c*) Ignorance
(*d*) Proudness
(*e*) Selfishness
(*f*) Extreme passion
(*g*) Excessive hope and desire
(*h*) Depression

- Achievements : (*a*) Truth
(*b*) Disciplinary beauty
(*c*) Fearlessness
(*d*) controlling power
(*e*) Spiritual flight
(*f*) Flow of potentiality
(*g*) Sacrifice
(*h*) Sound health
- Meditation can be done two times in a day. One is the morning at 7 o'clock. One at night at 7 o'clock. But one who wants to meditate only one time he or she should do it in the morning at 7 o'clock.

PECULIARITIES OF TANTRIC RULES

Nepalese tantric rules and capacities solely and wholly depend upon secret religious spiritual spell. In Hindu and Buddhist religions there are many such tantric spells that in the practice for certain periods or time regularly and sincerely can be applied successfully for useful actions or evil actions in human life. Most of the religious secret ritual spells are made to apply for good purpose to provide happiness in human life. But narrow minded and wicked minded persons please the gods and goddesses of power and get boon of evil power from them to pour it in human life and create pain and problem for them. Such evil power used for evil actions by wicked minded persons cause much unseen problem and pain as well as unknown diseases that could not be cured and solved with the help of modern popular medicines. So such diseases need tantric healing. So people who heal diseases of the people tantrically using various powerful secret ritual spells apply them properly and give relief to the patients. Similar is the case of creating pain and problem in human life by wicked and selfish persons. They use various evil secret ritual spells to pour evil and harmful power in the human body to make persons suffer from mysterious unknown diseases. Such wicked and selfish persons enjoy much when they get success in creating lot of miseries in the life of the people. They plunder lot of joy in life when they hear sobbing, moaning of people due to pain and problems. Each and every rules or codes whether they are made to provide happiness or misery have their own peculiarities. All peculiarities are secret and ritual peculiarities. Those peculiarities are listed below to make know other people.

(*a*) All ritual secret rules or codes are formulated addressing gods and goddesses of power.

(*b*) Secret rules are not be spelled loudly in public when they are used for some purposes.

(*c*) Different gods and goddesses of power have different power. Such power is used for formulation of secret ritual spells coated with various power of secrecy.

(*d*) Most of the secret ritual spells or rules of power begin with 'Om' and end with 'Hum Fata' such beginning and ending of secret ritual rules of power mostly belong to Hindu religion.

(*e*) Again some ritual rules of power begin with 'Shree' and end with the pronunciation 'Namo'

(*f*) Such secret ritual spells or rules are given special name I mean religious name. It is known as 'Mantra'

(*g*) Such secret ritual rules of tantrism should be pronounced silently by closing eyes. What is pronounced can't be heard by other people.

(*h*) Most of these secret ritual rules of tantrism are the composition of seven holy letters. But some Mantras are composed of nine to eleven letters.

(*i*) All Mantras are made or composed in the name of gods and goddesses of power. Those Mantras are spelled silently but quite sincerely and attentively to draw the divine power in the speller.

(*j*) Virtuous and good secret spells are spelled by virtuous persons as monks, sages, hermits, priests etc. to do healing work for suffering persons. But bad and harmful secret ritual spells are spelled by evil and harmful persons such as witches wizards and other wicked minded persons with a view to cause pain and problem upon other persons.

(*k*) To hold such Mantras or to implement such secret ritual spells persons should concentrate their mind and closing their eyes. They should focus their attention to when the spell is thrown. So meditation is the correct way to implement Mantras.

(l) Various Mantras of various capacities and dimensions should be used in the practice in different ways following all required conditions other wise they will not be effective.

All these peculiarities of secret ritual spells or Mantras belong to Hindu religion and some of them belong to Buddhism. With the help of meditation persons perform these Mantras to gain divine power to combat with evil spirits and black spirits and vice-versa Regular practice of these rules or Mantras make persons quite perfect and become expert in this field. These secret ritual rules or Mantras are spelled secretly by persons in the morning and night time. After getting up in the morning and before going to bed at night time. These two times are quite suitable time to meditate Mantras.

If monks, sages, hermits, priests etc. have to use these secret ritual rules or Mantras for healing disease they can use them at any time to get the patients or sufferers free from evil spirit and all kinds of black harmful spirits. In rural parts of Nepal Dhame and Jhakre are persons who are considered as users of such Mantras to treat the patients of unknown and complicated diseases caused by evil and harmful spirits. Majority of the people of Nepal have believed that most of the unknown and complicated diseases are caused by witches or wizards. But such diseases can be caused by other kinds of bad and black evil spirits such as ghosts, fantoms skeltonic figure and khyak.

All Mantras that have mentioned peculiarities belong to Hindu religion and some of them belong to Buddhism. They are often used as healing religious rules or mantras. As Mantras have practical use they are known as codes of tantrism such tantric codes or laws are used in Nepal from the time immemorial. But my own rule for curing the unknown diseases or complications, pain and problems occurring in human life because of evil spirits and the black spirits is quite different

from those old Mantras. In my rule seven letters that are not familiar to other persons are enough to face or cure any kinds of mysterious and unknown diseases, pain and problems. Those letters are in all cases whether they are mild one or hard one would be used to cure the diseases and to put away any kinds of pain and problems. These seven letters are used in different ways in different cases. Those secret ritual spells of Hindu religion and other religions are not taken in my tantric healing. As in my tantric action there are four kinds of Mandalas that I have presented in this book and these seven letters also are used mainly in four different ways as shown in the Mandalas. The complete frame work or structure of my tantrism is fixed in these seven letters. I have already mentioned above some where in this book that the real meaning of these letters.

I AM SAFE

Here safe is safe from all kinds of evil spirits and all kinds of harmful black spirits. I know and I want to make know other people of other countries of the world that in Nepal about ninty percent of the people living in rural parts of the country are illiterate that's why they believe in god and in evil spirits. When some things occur in their life they would think that the occurance is either due to god or due to evil spirits. Because of such belief in superstition people are suffering unnaturally. In the urban side of the country because of high influence of education they began to change in their thinking. Their blind belief or superstition also is decreasing every year yet urban people also have believed in useful and harmful super beings. About fifty present of urban people believe that the evil spirits and other harmful spirits have made them suffering from unknown diseases. They believe that such diseases can be healed not by the physician but by the sages, monks, hermits, Dhami, Jhakre etc. and used to rush to them for quick healing. So they would rush to the healers to get relief from such evil spirits. From such treatment for the sufferers of Nepal it has been clear that people have given preference to tantric treatment. It has been so because of so many reasons. People of Nepal are poor, illiterate, ignorant, belief in superstition, high fate in religion etc. are the main factors responsible for their preference to such treatment. Another cause of going to tantric healers is it is easy to reach to healers. In fact, religion and science both are abstract and uneasy subjects to understand for ordinary people. People of ordinary nature do not know how evil spirits and black spirits reach in human dwellings. Similarly they do not even know how various activities or events appear on the screen of television. Most of the religious and scientific activities of the people are abstract and mysterious for common people. That's why people turned to religion and believed in tantrism for religion is closely linked with human life since the time immemorial than to believe in science and its activities. But in fact both religion and science must go hand in hand for tasting sweet and pure harmony in people. Both subjects religion and science have their own speciality, strength value, ways of actions. Both must be embraced by the people in equal level to enjoy all available benefits of the Earth being free from all kinds of human weakness, being free from fear of evil spirits and other harmful spirits. The practical side of both religion and science must be evaluated in the real taste of human life of the Earth. Those will be quite happy soul of the Earth who use both tantrism and science in equal length. One sided people between these two poles can't be successful in life rather they will be just like rigid vertical people that can't be bent though they are heated in religions or scientific furnace.

GLOSSARY

Fantom : A shadowy illusive evil figure.
Gonam : A unclear illusive evil spirit.
Sage : A pious religious person of high knowledge of religion.
Monk : Priest or religious person.
Dhami : A healer of evil spirit and black spirit.
Jhakre : A healer of bad, black and evil spirit.
Khyak : A black human sized harmful illusive figure.
Dharmasala : A pubic free lodge for travellers.
Jantra : A ritually prepared thing of power to hang round the neck or to bind round the waist.
Jal : Ritually spilled holy water to be used as medicine.
Bibhuti : Ash prepared ritually to mark on the forehead.
Prabhu : A person of high religious calebre.
Guru : Teacher or preacher.
Hom : A grand ritual religious performance.
Maha Kali : A female highly powerful Goddess.
Kitchkani : A beautiful young female evil spirit whose feet is opposite to normal woman.
Kawancha : A harmful evil bony spirit.
Bhuta : Evil spirit that causes famine by consuming food.
Preta : Evil figure or spirit that causes unbearable pain and anxiety.
Mantra : Secret ritual spell.
Yogya : Religious performance done to please gods and goddesses.
Gaanja : Raw narcotic thing use as smoking.

Bhajan : A group song of religious praying.

Maha Deva : A God of high power of Hinduism that stands for human welfare.

Lord Krishna : God of high power of Hindu religion who stands for justice and human welfare.

Lord Ganesh : God of benevolence, good fortune and good time.

Mata : Mother.

Shree Panchami : A special festive day to worship Goddess Sarashowti, a Goddess of learning.

Laxmi Pooja : A special festive day to worship Goddess of wealth.

Look Maha Deve : Hidden Maha Deva God in the ground.

Ardha Nareshwor : Half male and half female God.

TaitisKoti Devata : Thirty three hundreds millions Gods and Goddesses.

Maha Kal : God superior to death God.

Karkot Naga : Powerful snake God.

Manakamana Mai : Mother Goddess that fulfil human desire.

Yana : Doctrine

Viskchhu : Buddhist monk or sage

Damaru : A mini two sided, drum like religious instrument to use in time of worshipping.

Sanakha : A religious holy water pouring means

Bajra : A religious hand handling in time of worshipping.

Sukunda : A religious holy lamp to burn in religious performances.

Thanka : A hanging religious picture of Gods and Goddesses.

Dholak : A two sided drum like instrument.

Tinchhu : A pair of round small ringing instrument made of metal.

Trisul : Three bladed religious weapon to use upon other rival figure.

Kaa : A pair of long musical instrument to be played in time religious function.

Mukha : A special religious cap to put on in religious performance.

Chhatra : A religious umbrella to be used for Gods and Goddesses.

Muralee : Lute.

Khadga : Two bladed weapon pointed at the top.

Gulpa : A round small pot to put rice grain.

Jolanhakan : A flat and pointed at the top religious thing to use as mirror.

Dalu : A hanging religious lamp.

Shenamu : An artistic pot made of metal to use as putting colour pest to mark on forehead.

Kalas : A water pot made of metal.

Pujava : A plate to use for putting worshipping material.

Patra : A pointed round flat pot to be used in religious performance.

Pujari : Worshipper and care taker of Gods and goddesses and their temple.

Dwar Pal : Gate keeper of the temple.

Bhairab : A hindu God of power.

Kumari : A living Goddess of hindus.

Kumari Ghar : Home of Living Goddess Kumari.

Tika : A red pest to mark on the forehead as sign of good luck or fortune.

Jamana Gubhaju : The greatest tantric person of Nepal who never ate rice.

Dyoma : A woman of divine power supposed as goddess mother.

Dyomaiju : An unmarried girl of divine power.

Parvati : Goddess of high tantric power of Hindu religion.

Sita : Goddess of purity and perseverance of hindu religion.

Radha : Goddess of simplicity and love of hind religion.

Durga : Goddess of high power who stands for human welfare.

Mandala : A religious picture of significance to be used for worshipping.

Mandap : A religious place or seat to be used for religious purpose as meditation, worshipping, Hom etc.